Chasing Intimacy

AL NOVAK

WESTBOW
PRESS®
A DIVISION OF THOMAS NELSON
& ZONDERVAN

Copyright © 2022 Al Novak.

All rights reserved. No part of this book may be used or reproduced by any means, graphic, electronic, or mechanical, including photocopying, recording, taping or by any information storage retrieval system without the written permission of the author except in the case of brief quotations embodied in critical articles and reviews.

This book is a work of non-fiction. Unless otherwise noted, the author and the publisher make no explicit guarantees as to the accuracy of the information contained in this book and in some cases, names of people and places have been altered to protect their privacy.

WestBow Press books may be ordered through booksellers or by contacting:

WestBow Press
A Division of Thomas Nelson & Zondervan
1663 Liberty Drive
Bloomington, IN 47403
www.westbowpress.com
844-714-3454

Because of the dynamic nature of the Internet, any web addresses or links contained in this book may have changed since publication and may no longer be valid. The views expressed in this work are solely those of the author and do not necessarily reflect the views of the publisher, and the publisher hereby disclaims any responsibility for them.

Any people depicted in stock imagery provided by Getty Images are models, and such images are being used for illustrative purposes only. Certain stock imagery © Getty Images.

ISBN: 978-1-6642-5789-4 (sc)
ISBN: 978-1-6642-5790-0 (hc)
ISBN: 978-1-6642-5788-7 (e)

Library of Congress Control Number: 2022902865

Print information available on the last page.

WestBow Press rev. date: 3/16/2022

Scripture taken from the New King James Version® Copyright © 1982 by Thomas Nelson. Used by permission. All rights reserved.

[Scripture quotations are] from the New Revised Standard Version Bible, copyright © 1989 the Division of Christian Education of the National Council of the Churches of Christ in the United States of America. Used by permission. All rights reserved.

Scripture quotations taken from The Holy Bible, New International Version® NIV® Copyright © 1973 1978 1984 2011 by Biblica, Inc. TM. Used by permission. All rights reserved worldwide.

Scripture taken from the King James Version of the Bible.

Scripture quotations taken from the (NASB®) New American Standard Bible®, Copyright © 1960, 1971, 1977, 1995, 2020 by The Lockman Foundation. Used by permission. All rights reserved. www.lockman.org

Scripture quotations marked (NLT) are taken from the Holy Bible, New Living Translation, copyright ©1996, 2004, 2015 by Tyndale House Foundation. Used by permission of Tyndale House Publishers, a Division of Tyndale House Ministries, Carol Stream, Illinois 60188. All rights reserved.

Scripture taken from The Message. Copyright © 1993, 1994, 1995, 1996, 2000, 2001, 2002. Used by permission of NavPress Publishing Group.

Scripture taken from the Amplified Bible, Copyright © 1954, 1958, 1962, 1964, 1965, 1987 by The Lockman Foundation. Used with permission.

Scripture quotations are from the ESV® Bible (The Holy Bible, English Standard Version®), copyright © 2001 by Crossway, a publishing ministry of Good News Publishers. Used by permission. All rights reserved.

To my wife, Terri, and our children and their spouses, grandchildren, and all our future generations to come and particularly all those seeking intimacy with God.

Contents

Foreword xi
Introduction xv
Preface xvii

Chapter 1	The Chase 1
Chapter 2	Early Co-Op Childhood 10
Chapter 3	Orchard Lake Days 18
Chapter 4	Hello, Girls! 29
Chapter 5	Honeymoon Nightmare 37
Chapter 6	A Cop's Life 43
Chapter 7	God, Please Help Me! 50
Chapter 8	God Sends Help 52
Chapter 9	Acupuncture 56
Chapter 10	The Problems Increase 61
Chapter 11	God Sends an Angel? 64
Chapter 12	Have You Heard? 67
Chapter 13	Have You Asked? 70
Chapter 14	Candy Van 79
Chapter 15	Explaining It to Terri 86
Chapter 16	Christian Cops Meet 91
Chapter 17	Testing Begins 95
Chapter 18	Smoking Obstacle 100
Chapter 19	The Peace of God 107

Chapter 20	Coping with Tragedies	111
Chapter 21	Booze Beginnings	116
Chapter 22	Rookie Acceptance	122
Chapter 23	The Human Body	128
Chapter 24	Bloom Where You Are Planted!	133
Chapter 25	Sliding into Legalism	139
Chapter 26	Career Change	142
Chapter 27	FMM Possibilities	148
Chapter 28	Jail Beginnings	153
Chapter 29	New Jail Transition	163
Chapter 30	Chaplaincy Classes	167
Chapter 31	The Wisdom of Marilyn	174
Chapter 32	Moving into Grace	177
Chapter 33	Our First Housing Miracle	186
Chapter 34	Experiencing God	191
Chapter 35	Miracle Dog	194
Chapter 36	Performance Theology	199
Chapter 37	Jail Ministry Grows	204
Chapter 38	Prayer Team	212
Chapter 39	"Al, I Got Your Back"	225
Chapter 40	Back to Intimacy	233

Conclusion	237
About the Author	245

Foreword

When asked to write a foreword for this book, I contemplated what I should write about. After reading Al's manuscript, I found that I was on a roller coaster ride to my own past. And we will start there.

Several years have passed since personally retiring from the police department. Al's stories and remembrances stirred some old emotions, both good and bad. As a cop, one must be able to repress the evil of the moment to live a semblance of normal life, whatever that is in our times.

A short history lesson defines the word "cop". It was initially an acronym for English police officers that were first formed by Sir Robert Peel in London. And yes, they were called Sir Bobby Peel's Metro, or Bobbies. When the officer received an assignment for duty, they chalked their names on a board entitled "Constable on Patrol" or cop. So, the word cop has a very positive beginning and distinguished heritage.

Often, we see crimes on tv and observe lots of violence, but it is only on a screen set before us. Cops must pick up the pieces they see in the real world and set forth mechanisms to repress their emotions before they head home to their families.

Al Novak opened wide some of my old emotions in his book, some being good and some being bad, but he is straightforward. He covered them quite succinctly and graphically. So, we will let the book speak for itself. If you want to know what a police officer thinks in most cases, read the book. If you want to know what family life is like for a police officer, read the book. If you want to know why a cop reacts as they do, read the book. And if you want to know what Jesus can do for any person, read the book.

Jesus watched over me for nearly thirty years of policework. I have continued to trust Him to see me through to the end. Jesus also watched over Al while guiding him to his next work. I remember the day very well when he made the announcement that he was leaving the police department and the very words he used when he declared his intent.

We were on patrol heading north on Woodward Avenue near Normandy Road in Royal Oak when, out of the blue, Al says, "Randy, I made a decision. I am leaving police work."

I asked him, "Why, what brought this about?"

He replied, and get this, "I'm tired of dealing with these people, the ones you arrest day after day. They are back out on the street before you finish writing the report. I don't ever want to see another jail cell." Well, we know now that was not God's plan.

If you want to know how Jesus can change your life, read the book.

Randy Young (a.k.a. Doc Young)
Christiankarate.net
Biblebasics.us

In this book you'll meet a man who has spent a lifetime pondering and reflecting upon the way his life relates to the person and work of Jesus Christ. Not everyone's journey to Christian faith will resemble my father's, but no matter who you are, you will be moved, surprised, and challenged by the faith expressed in the stories of this book. As one of his children, I can tell you that this book accurately and passionately portrays the type of faith my dad holds dear, a rich faith that has been the subject of many long (and sometimes enthusiastic) discussions over the decades. I treasure this book because it honestly and humbly reveals to any reader the father I've been blessed to call, "Dad." Read this book!

Rev. Dr. Joseph Novak, pastor
First Presbyterian Church of Flint

Introduction

How many people say they believe in God? How many of those would say they have an intimate relationship with God in Christ? Do they even know what that means? Satan believes in God and even had an intimate relationship with Him at one point.

In Chasing Intimacy, Al touches on what true intimacy with God looks and feels like. It is not religion, it is not performance, it is love. It is resting in the knowledge that no matter what we face in this life, God really does have our back when we put our complete trust in Him. This however requires intimacy with our heavenly Father.

Al shares a lifelong journey that started in a very intimate way but veered off course for many reasons that we can all relate to only to come back to where he started.

The testimony is powerful, honest, and sincere. It also speaks to God's grace and mercy and His willingness to accept us just as we are no matter our past. This is a grace that gives all that trust in Him a genuine peace that truly passes all understanding.

Dr. Thomas Saunders, PhD.
Pastor
Author of "Choices"
Co-Author of "The Road Between us the Elder and the Atheist"

Preface

Most of us just want to know the truth in life. Our main discussion topics generally are religion, politics, family, and friendships. Generally, we will disagree with one another on most topics since there seems to be no central place to find absolute or factual truth. If you search the media, you will only get opinions with little or mostly biased truth. Even when you search the scriptures, interpretations from various scholars will cloud the truth. So, what can one believe is the absolute truth?

Jesus said He was the truth in John 14. I believe that Jesus was correct. There is no variation on this—no matter what others may claim. Jesus set an example for us followers as He would often, according to the scriptures, amid ministry activity, leave and go to be alone with his Father.

Throughout my spiritual life journeys, I began to wonder why Jesus did that. There must be a reason, and I contemplated this often. After realizing that most Christians were just connecting with God on the surface, like I was, a reason emerged to write this book. A genuine desire surfaced in my heart to share with my fellow believers what I had discovered: that God truly has more of Him waiting for us to discover. Knowing God our Father (our Dad in heaven) in a much deeper and more intimate way is the focus of this book.

I once heard a message from a preacher who said, "Imagination is the portal into the spiritual realm."

At first, I cringed at that statement since I believe that truth comes from the Bible itself. Later thinking his statement through, I had to agree that we really do think in pictures (images). So, having the right image or photo of God, since He describes Himself as a Spirit, became a new entryway into deeper spiritual exploration.

> Philip said to (Jesus), "Lord, show us the Father, and we will be satisfied." Jesus said, "Have I been with you all this time, Philip, and you still do not know me? Whoever has seen me has seen the Father. How can you say, 'Show us the Father'?" John 14:9 (NRSV)

My desire was to put the puzzle pieces together, and this required most of my life as I personally chased after this intimacy with God.

This intimacy was there at the very beginning when I cried out to Him for the first time. I learned that religion and its works system can detour that relationship. May the reader find a genuine craving to have more intimate time with God as the pages turn in this book.

During my growing-up years, my seventeen-year police career, and my thirty-three years as a jail chaplain all became days, months, and years of discovery. I learned that God genuinely desires and wants intimacy with us. He created us to know, love, and serve Him, and knowing Him means intimately.

My hope for this book is to aid the body of Christ in finding genuine intimacy with God: our "heavenly Dad." May you climb up into His lap and sense and feel His presence, security, and plenty of big hugs as you read this book.

Al Novak

CHAPTER 1

The Chase

It was a clear, crisp morning as I walked out the back door of the Royal Oak Police Headquarters. I was assigned squad car 802 that morning. It was Sunday morning, and most often, it would be a quiet morning with maybe a report or two. Sundays were a special day for me since I usually would tune in to my favorite preachers on the AM radio in my police cruiser. Since I usually rode alone, the radio choices were up to me. I liked riding alone, and most of my fellow officers preferred it that way—that is, me riding alone—since I had become a Christian. My brothers in blue had a hard time accepting my newly found Christian faith, and truthfully, they didn't want to know much about it. I guess I was partially responsible since I kind of shoved it down their throats, but it wasn't intentional. I found myself being quite enthusiastic about my faith in Christ, and I lived it openly. I guess their real beef was that I didn't seem to fit in anymore with the guys, and they were right. Living in Christ makes one seem as though fitting in is impossible—except with other Christians.

The restaurant that morning wasn't too busy. The church crowd hadn't arrived yet, and I really preferred it that way. I didn't like to sit in a crowded restaurant wearing my uniform because people always seemed to gawk at me. Most uniformed police officers experience "fishbowlitis" wherever they are, especially in restaurants.

During my coffee breaks, I would usually sit at the counter and read my Bible. Perusing through a psalm or reading through a chapter in Proverbs was a great place to start the day. Quite often, in the morning, some street drunk would stumble into the restaurant and sit down next to me. It was always interesting to watch their response when they observed me reading the Bible.

The conversation would go something like this.

"How ya doin', Officer?"

"Fine," I would answer. "How are you?"

"Oh, a little rugged, I guess," he would say as his hands shook.

"Rough night last night?"

He'd then give a half-effort chuckle. He would always glance down at my Bible sitting in front of me on the counter next to my coffee and ask, "Whatcha readin'?"

I would smile and tell him about what I was just reading in my Bible—no matter where I was at—and then I would begin to share my faith with him.

Some of these people would gulp down their coffee, even though it was very hot, toss some coins on the counter, and go away, but some would ask more questions.

As my coffee break ended, I would give them a tract and ask them to consider Christ. I would shake their hands, tell them that God loves them, and say that I hoped to see them again. Some would wag their heads in disbelief as I walked away. Some of the patrons who overheard our conversations would shift about in their seats and look away.

It was time for some of my favorite Sunday-morning preachers to air. Dr. J. Vernon McGee would broadcast his *Sunday Sermon,* and I didn't want to miss it. Local station WEXL AM 1430 was tuned in as I called back into service and continued my patrol duties. After a few routine calls—a noise complaint (a dog was barking and disturbing a neighbor who wanted to sleep in because it was Sunday morning), an abandoned auto (I marked the tire for a twenty-four-hour check back), and a larceny report (a man had two hubcaps stolen off his car in his driveway during the night)—it seemed like a typical Sunday tour of duty.

At eleven o'clock every Sunday morning, a local Baptist congregation aired their morning worship service live. I liked to hear the preacher speak since I thought he was a good speaker. He was very articulate and had very thought-provoking messages. Little did I know that day, as I listened to that preacher's sermon, that God would interweave our lives a bit more personally.

As the preacher was delivering his sermon on the air, a young Black man entered the rear lobby of the church. He asked the ushers standing in the back if they had a phone.

They told him that there was a pay phone downstairs.

He asked if they could loan him twenty cents for a phone call.

They cordially gave it to him, and he thanked them as he walked down the steps to the telephone. Little did the ushers know that he had previously hot-wired the pastor's car and had it idling in the drive just outside the door.

When he got downstairs, rather than making a phone call, he grabbed an armful of coats off the coatrack next to the pay phone and walked back upstairs. He excused himself, brushing by the ushers and deacons standing by the door, tossed the coats in the back seat of the pastor's car, and drove away.

One of the deacons who happened to be an auxiliary police officer with our department started to put things mentally together. "That looks like the pastor's car!" he said.

"Hey, that guy just stole the pastor's car—and our coats," one of the ushers said.

"Call the police," said another.

I was sitting at the light on the corner of Fourth and Main Street. A high-pitched radio tone was transmitted indicating a BOL broadcast ("be on the lookout") broadcast was about to air. The dispatcher said, "BOL for a late-model Ford, two-tone brown in color, driven by a Black male occupant. Last seen heading southbound on Rochester Road"— radio squelch— "occupant believed to have stolen this vehicle and coats from Central Free Will Baptist Church"—radio squelch— "vehicle may belong to Pastor Milton Worthington."

As the dispatch was being aired, I looked up and observed a two-tone brown Ford sedan with a Black male occupant traveling south through the intersection. Proceeding quickly southbound, I was able to catch up to the vehicle and transmitted the plate number to headquarters. A L.E.I.N. (AKA Law Enforcement Information Network) check was made to see who owned the vehicle. Within minutes, the information was relayed back to me that the vehicle belonged to Milton Worthington. I was also given his full address. I informed the station that I was following the vehicle southbound on Main Street, heading toward our city limits at Ten Mile.

I radioed to our neighboring suburb, Pleasant Ridge PD and asked for a roadblock to be set up as I was approaching their city limits. They were a smaller city and only had two available squad cars to send. Both Pleasant Ridge officers placed themselves near the center of Main Street, which was wide and consisted of six lanes. The officers were behind their cars, waving to the driver of the stolen vehicle to stop his vehicle, as I pulled in behind him with my overhead lights turned on. I assumed that the suspect saw the escape route around the police cars, and sure enough, he took off. Engaging my lights and siren, I began to pursue him.

Main Street intersected on an angle leading into Woodward Avenue, which was four lanes northbound and four lanes southbound, divided by a median. The fleeing suspect ran both lights on a dead red while crossing four northbound lanes. Following behind him, we both were now traveling more than seventy miles per hour. Weaving in and out of traffic, covering all four southbound lanes, the pursuit continued with the siren of car 802 undulating up and down.

I radioed ahead to Ferndale PD, the next city suburb that we were about to enter. Roadblocks were set up at Nine Mile Road. This time, as we both approached at high rates of speed, all four lanes were blocked with traffic backed up and several Ferndale cars sitting in the middle of the intersection. There were twelve-inch-high cement curbs on both sides of Woodward Avenue. The only possible escape route was between a fire hydrant and a telephone pole on the right—if one could get over the curb.

The fleeing Ford sedan hit the curb and went airborne, landing just between the two objects. It fishtailed to the left and then back into the intersection, where Ferndale officers were standing behind their squad cars with shotguns.

Bam! Bam! Buckshot penetrated the metal skin of the car as it passed by the officers. The shots were placed at the front part of the driver's door, just missing the driver. I managed to squeeze my squad car through the narrow opening, and the pursuit continued southbound with other police cars following behind us.

Continuously, I radioed my location to our dispatcher as we weaved our way through traffic at ninety to one hundred miles per hour. The next major intersection was Eight Mile Road. This was the beginning of the Detroit city limits. The fleeing driver blew through the red lights facing all four lanes westbound and then all four lanes eastbound of Eight Mile Road. Braking my way through the intersections, I was able to swerve and avoid several collisions as I crossed the lanes behind him. After getting through the eastbound lanes and finally being able to look up, he was gone.

He had completely disappeared! The brakes on my squad car smelled like they were burning up as I came to a screeching stop.

A man holding onto a street sign pole, reminding me of the proverbial drunk hanging on a light post, started hollering at me and pointing down the side street that I had just passed. "Offisher, Offisher, he went thataway!"

I backed up and proceeded quickly westbound down the side street that the drunk had pointed to. Looking from side to side through the driveways of houses that lined the street, I continued down the street, but I saw nothing.

Suddenly, out of my left-side peripheral vision, I caught a red taillight in an alleyway behind one of the houses on my left. I quickly found a drive to enter the alley, all the while radioing information to other assisting police vehicles. Looking down the alley, off in the far distance, I saw some car taillights. Could it be our fleeing suspect?

Pushing my foot on the accelerator pedal, the transmission popped into passing gear as I sped down the narrow alleyway, which ended into the parking lot of St. John the Baptist, Byzantine Rite Catholic Church. Ahead of me, the fleeing suspect jumped out of the stolen car and took off running back toward Woodward Avenue. The Ferndale cars were arriving, and officers were running in every direction. I came running up behind him, and we had him surrounded. Shotguns and pistols were all aimed at the suspect since this was a felony in progress.

He looked around and finally stopped. It was over; he gave up.

His hands went up, and he was ordered to the ground. He was face down on the ground as I began to handcuff him. The customary Miranda warnings (his right to remain silent, anything said will be used against him in court, and his right to an attorney) were recited to him audibly from memory.

To make matters worse, I looked up and noticed that the church was letting out.

A man from the church walked up to me with an unwrapped loaf of bread as I was in the process of handcuffing the prisoner. He said, "Officer, I am from St. John the Baptist Catholic Church here. I am supposed to give this loaf of bread to the first person I see—and you are the first person."

My heart was fiercely pulsating, and I was nearly breathless as I was securing my prisoner. "Excuse me sir," I said. "Would you just wait one minute until I get this fellow over to my squad car?"

He said, "Sure, Officer," and he just stood there as I escorted my prisoner to the back seat of my car.

Police officers were arriving from everywhere. The TV2 news team from Detroit arrived and began to ask me questions. I could not believe that a film crew could be that fast to the scene.

I asked, "How on earth did you get here so fast?"

The reporter told me that they were sitting in a restaurant at Nine Mile Road when they saw the chase go right by in front of them. The entire film crew began to follow us and had just arrived.

I walked back to the man with the loaf of bread and said, "OK, sir, now what were you saying about me being the first person for what?"

He told me that his church had a special service that day reflecting on the feeding of the hungry by giving a loaf of bread to the first person they saw after they left the church. From the church steps, he saw me wrestling with a man on the ground and decided that I was the one. He handed me the loaf of bread.

I graciously thanked him and then answered some questions for the news reporter as my fellow officers arrived from Royal Oak and began the procedure for impounding the car. I radioed my dispatcher that I would be "ten-fifteen" (en route to the station with a prisoner). I started back toward the Royal Oak Police station with my prisoner handcuffed in the back seat.

I glanced in my rearview mirror and could see his eyes.

He looked out the window off and on and he seemed to be psychologically aware of his situation. He looked like he had been toughened through the struggles of life, yet he appeared almost as though he was thankful to be caught.

I asked him, "Do you think anyone has been praying for you?" This was an unusual way to begin a conversation with a newly handcuffed prisoner, but I was thinking of how many lives had been endangered during that chase and how he miraculously avoided any serious injury.

He responded, "Yes."

I asked, "Who?"

He answered, "My grandma."

I asked him, "How do you know that?"

He said, "She has always prayed for me."

Responding back, "Do you believe that God heard her prayers today by saving your life?"

"Yes, sir."

"Is your grandma a Christian?"

He nodded his head up and down.

"Do you think that your grandma has been praying for you to become a Christian also?"

"I know she has," he said. "She told me that she was praying that I would become a Christian."

I said to him, "I am a Christian. God permitted me to catch you today to tell you that He loves you very much. He sent His Son, Jesus Christ, to die upon a cross for you." I shared with him several verses from the Bible:

> "For God so loved the world, that he gave his only begotten Son, that whosoever believeth in him should not perish, but have everlasting life." John 3:16 (KJV)

> "For the Son of man is come to seek and to save that which was lost." Luke 19:10 (KJV)

I said to him, "Today, the Son of Man has sought after you to save you from the lake of fire. He must love you very much to save you from not only physical death but spiritual death as well. Would you like to receive Jesus Christ as your personal Savior right now?"

He looked up with tears streaming down his face and said, "Yes I do, Officer."

I told him that he needed to pray with all his heart and ask Jesus Christ to be his Savior. I told him to ask God for forgiveness and ask Him to take charge over his life. And there in the back seat of car 802, my prisoner, who was weeping before God, asked—sincerely with his own words—for God to save him.

En route to the station, I shared some of my personal testimony of how I came to know Jesus as my Savior. After the booking procedure at the police station, I walked him down the hallway to his cell.

He stopped and thanked me with tears in his eyes as I handed him a Bible to read. He thanked me several more times.

I could tell that he was a different person. His heart had been changed forever by God's grace when he placed his faith in our wonderful Lord Jesus Christ:

> Amazing Grace, how sweet the sound, that saved a wretch like me. I once was lost but now am found, was blind but now I see.

> "For by grace you have been saved through faith, and that not of yourselves; it is the gift of God, not of works, lest anyone should boast." Ephesians 2:8-9 (NKJV)

CHAPTER 2

Early Co-Op Childhood

My childhood days were spent in the co-op. Let me explain. I was born on May 4, 1945. My brother Joe was eight years older, and my brother Gary was four years older. My mom, after having two sons, desperately wanted a daughter. All my aunts, uncles, family, and friends assured my mom that I would be a girl—everyone except my grandpa (Mom's father), Albert Kalinin. My parents, Joseph and Mary, (sounds like a biblical family) were hoping that my grandpa was wrong. Well, after my birth, my mom reluctantly named me Albert after her dad. Albert is a name of nobility and means "illustrious," which I frequently share with others and get a laugh.

In frustration, my mom decided she would raise me like a girl. So, I became very attached to my mother's apron strings. She taught me how to cook like her mother taught her, clean the kitchen and house, and do all the things a mother would teach a daughter. Wherever my mom was, her son (or imaginary daughter)

Albert was right there. Yeah, my brothers were generally outside playing baseball, football, golf, or horseshoes, and I was learning how to cook and clean and sew.

It was very hard being so attached to my mother. It was very terrifying to consider going to school and leaving my mom for even one day. Kindergarten was a real challenge, and my mother cried all day when I had to go to school. I cried as much as she did, and I would try to hide my tears. I was scared about being away from her; kindergarten was a real adjustment for me.

After the Second World War ended, my parents lived in a government housing project called Parkside in Detroit. My dad was a jack-of-all-trades. He was an overhead crane operator in the Hudson and Packard car factories and learned to be a bricklayer. Other families in the projects had fathers who were skilled tradesmen, and they decided to get together and form a group called "The Co-Operative Homesteads" (AKA Co-Op). The group pooled all their resources, borrowed what they could, and purchased a 140-acre parcel in Royal Oak Township, which was later situated in the incorporated city of Madison Heights.

Individual families purchased at least one acre from Co-Operative Homesteads and pledged to build their house on it. Each of the Co-Op members would contribute their unique skills and help their neighbors build their own homes. The only way they could afford a house was by reducing their construction labor costs on each home. Those were hard times, but my dad and the Co-Op folks, over a period of years, built our cinder block home in this rural farming community.

They also contacted and met with an architect by the name of Frank Lloyd Wright for his suggestions about solar types of house construction. Mr. Wright later became a well-known and worldwide-acclaimed architect. He came out to visit with our group and made several suggestions for solar houses with very large front glass windows facing south to supplement heating costs. Many of the folks who built homes there followed several of his suggestions. The streets were later named after him: Frank Avenue, Lloyd Avenue, and Wright Avenue. My dad built his house on 670 Lloyd Avenue.

The idea was great, and each person committed to helping their neighbors during the construction process of their homes. My dad supplied his bricklayer skills to the homes that were constructed with cinder and cement blocks and those having brick veneer during those early years of building homes in the Co-Op. Each neighbor was not able to work full-time on building each other's homes since everyone was employed somewhere else full-time to earn a living. So, most of the construction labor work was done in the evenings or on weekends.

My dad was very fussy and quite often would redo the work previously done by one of the Co-Op partners. Some of the workers were very skilled, but there were others who were not so adept who also contributed.

We initially lived in a small flat roofed garage-type unit as my dad continued for several years to build the main house in stages. Dad, along with the help of my two older brothers and our neighbors, spent all their extra time constructing the main house addition. I was about four years old when we moved from Detroit to the Co-Op. Despite being a mama's boy, my brothers tried to teach me sports stuff like baseball, football, golf, horseshoes, and hockey in the winter. We were required to work in the garden most of the summer as everyone in the Co-Op had a big garden to grow and can their own food. They nicknamed me "busybody" since I was a nosy kid and into everybody's business all the time.

My dad was a very funny storyteller and would bring our family to gut laughter when he would share his life experiences around the dinner table, which self-medicated our family. We learned to pursue laughter as the main course of our daily lives. God's perspective on this is shared in His Word:

> "A merry heart does good, like medicine." Proverbs 17:22 (NKJV)

My brother Joe always wanted me to play sports. He tried to teach me baseball, but I stunk at it. He coached my elementary football team at Guardian Angels Catholic School in Clawson. I was not a very good player since I was a scaredy-cat, and he pushed me day in and day out to perform. Sadly, I did not desire to play sports especially where I could get hurt. He worked my butt off in football practice, but I just wanted to be with my mother. Joe was the big brother every kid would love to have. He always took care of his younger brothers, and since he never married, he always took care of his nephews and nieces like his own children.

Joe was a postal carrier for many years and retired from the post office. He worked out of the Royal Oak Office. This was the post office where the term "going postal" was made infamous. In fact, Joe was working on November 14, 1991, the day of the nationally reported shooting. He told me that he was setting up his daily route at his station when he heard what sounded like gunshots. Employees were running all around and shouting, "Get out of here now!"

Tom McIlvane, the gunman, began a shooting spree after selecting his targets, mainly supervisors at the post office. He was angry that he had been turned down on an appeal to be reinstated as a carrier after he was fired for being insubordinate to a supervisor. Joe, looking for an escape, was able to climb through a side window, and he ran across the parking lot to a safer area. McIlvane killed four persons and wounded four others.

The disgruntled former postal carrier, after killing four persons, headed back to the postmaster's office, but he was unable to get the door open since the postmaster had locked the door after hearing the gunfire. The assailant then turned the gun on himself and committed suicide. Joe still has a hard time talking about the incident after all these years. He says that he really liked some of the supervisors who were killed. He thought they were very nice people with overall good hearts.

Joe is now eighty-four years old. Overall, his health is very good with some minor age-related issues even though he has yet to see any doctor. He faithfully walks one full hour every day, and he doesn't let the weather stop him. My brother still applies the famous postal carrier saying to his daily walking routine: "Neither snow nor rain nor heat nor gloom of night stays these couriers from the swift completion of their appointed rounds." Not so sure if this is true any longer.

My brother Gary taught me how to play golf. We used to set up an imaginary chipping course with a 9-iron from tree to pole to bush to marker. I got pretty good at my short game with all that practice. Across the road, there was a vacant large tract of land that had been shaped for a future housing development. Gary and I would go there two or three times a week and drive golf balls back and forth to one another all day long. My long game became pretty good as well, but I was not very good on the greens. I just couldn't get a read on the greens and often three-putted. Putting was my downfall in golf.

Gary was a gifted athlete. He could play just about any sport well. He pitched on a grade-school team, and the batters just couldn't hit him. He was that good. He was extremely good at golf and won the Red Run Golf Club (Royal Oak) caddy championship two years running. Gary was a master in chess. He also never married, and my brothers lived together in their later years as companions and best friends until Gary died in April 2019.

My life was pledged to be a mama's boy, but I did find a lifelong friend in one of our Co-Op neighbor's family. His name was Jerome

Brzezinski. The Brzezinski's had built their house in the Co-Op about a hundred yards south from us. Mr. Brzezinski was a skilled heating and refrigeration person. The Brzezinski's had formerly lived in Parkside also, and the youngest of their five children was Jerome. He was two years older than me, and we became best buddies and pals during my childhood and adolescence.

Mrs. Brzezinski was a committed and devout Roman Catholic. Most of the Catholic neighborhood kids were enrolled in Guardian Angels Parochial School in Clawson. I spent my first eight years attending Guardian Angels with several of the neighborhood kids. The elementary school was run by Dominican nuns. I received my First Communion at Guardian Angels and later completed all my catechism classes and was confirmed there as well. Baptism as a baby, Holy Communion at the age of reason, and confirmation were some of the sacraments practiced by Roman Catholics. Several of the neighbors and the Brzezinski family along with my family were Roman Catholics.

Jerome was being groomed by his mother for the priesthood. Mrs. B always wanted a priest in her family since her older brother was a monsignor and a parish priest up in Ludington, Michigan. Mrs. Brzezinski faithfully took us to Tuesday-evening Novena services at St. Mary's of Royal Oak, which offered a "plenary indulgence" if one completed all nine sessions. I must have completed at least five or more of these novenas simply to always be with my pal, Jerome.

A novena (from Latin: *novem*, "nine") is an ancient tradition of devotional praying in Christianity. It consists of private or public prayers repeated for nine successive days or weeks. In the Catholic tradition, much-used novena prayers include doctrinal statements in addition to personal petitions. A plenary indulgence is a remission before God of the entire temporal punishment due to sins (believed by Catholics) whose guilt had previously been forgiven through the Sacrament of Penance. A faithful Catholic who is duly disposed gains, under certain prescribed conditions through the action of the church, as the minister of redemption, dispenses and applies with authority the treasury of the satisfactions of Christ and the saints (OK, I don't fully get it other than the elimination of time to be spent in Purgatory which is believed to be a place of temporary punishment).

Growing up at the Brzezinski's was mostly fun, and I was often invited to vacation with them. I learned how to play pinochle with the family. Mr. Brzezinski counted cards and knew every card that I had in my hand. Jerome and I would often practice and play Mass in his basement. We acted out what the priest would do. We also played rough-and-tumble things outside. Jerome was my avenue to boyhood challenges. Growing up as a mama's boy made it difficult to associate with other boys. He and I would hang out in the woods and set up camp and even do some hunting with our BB guns. We were not troublesome kids, but we made some bad choices along the way.

On several occasions, I would borrow—also known as stealing—some of my dad's cigarettes and we would smoke them together at our campsite in the woods. Overall, we were just ordinary kids prone to trying out youthful things.

Jerome graduated from Guardian Angels and headed off to St. Mary's of Orchard Lake, an all-boys, boarding school that included a high school preparatory for college, a college, and seminary. It was a Polish American school that catered to those who considered themselves vocational students (or youths who desired to be Roman Catholic priests).

Believing that I also had a vocation to the priesthood, decided to follow in Jerome's footsteps two years later. My mom and dad could not afford to send me to Orchard Lake since it was eight hundred dollars per year, including room and board. Fr. Marcero at Guardian Angels talked my parents into sending me since I indicated that I believed that I had a vocation to be a priest. If it was God's call—we assumed that it was—my parents had no choice but to sacrifice and send me there. So, they did!

As a Catholic, I learned good, solid moral teachings. I learned that there was a God. I learned about Jesus and a Holy Spirit. I attended Mass every week and learned to reverence God. One of the instructions that always stuck with me was taught in one of the catechism classes that the whole purpose of man is to know, love, and serve God. I began to understand this to mean that my sole purpose was to know about God, love Him from a respectful distance, and serve Him. However, many years later my understanding of this teaching changed from "knowing about Him" to actually "knowing Him personally" and "loving Him" in an intimate deep personal way and that "serving Him" was simply the product of this intimate love relationship.

Jesus intimately prayed to His Father:

> "And this is eternal life, that they may know you, the only true God, and Jesus Christ whom you have sent." John 17:3 (NRSV)

CHAPTER 3

Orchard Lake Days

Jerome was a junior when I entered my freshman year at St. Mary's of Orchard Lake. I thought I would be able to be with him, but that wasn't going to happen. He had developed a totally different set of high school friends. We would see one another in passing occasionally, but I was basically alone with my new freshmen classmates and suffering with "mama's boy syndrome." It was time to grow up, and I am grateful for all my life-changing experiences at Orchard Lake. Oh, don't get me wrong. They were the most frightening days that a mama's boy and an introvert would ever want to experience. I was in the beginning stages of growing out of my boyhood into manhood, and I needed to stand up to some punishment on my own.

Today, disclosing some of these incidents might place some of these priest-teachers into some scrutiny. All my priest-instructors—we called them professors—have since died, and societal things were so different during those days. The acceptable discipline for an all-boys boarding school back then would most likely not be acceptable in today's educational spectrum. It was the right time for me to toughen up. I absolutely needed to grow up and found myself situated in the right spot.

During my freshman year at St. Mary's of Orchard Lake, all students were required to take eight classes per semester, including three languages: Polish, Latin, and English. We were required to attend study hall periods from seven to nine each weekday evening, which included some free study time periods (work quietly with a pal) and then attend strict study periods (work alone in silence) on our daily homework assignments.

Fr. Zdradowski taught freshmen religion. Like most of the priest-teachers who taught us, he was a firm instructor. A room full of high-energy adolescent teenage boys would necessitate a bit more understanding of their reasoning of disciplinary tactics.

Fr. Z was known by the boys as "pinhead" because he always had some hair on the back of his head that stood up. One day he announced to the class that we were going to have a test next week and that everybody had better get 100 percent on it. He carried a fiberglass rod that was wrapped and tightly wound with electrical tape. He used it as a blackboard pointer or sometimes a fencing type smacking rod, and it was often used simply as a disciplinary tool. He waved his rod in the air that day and said that everybody had better get a hundred on the test or else, pointing the rod of discipline directly at the class.

Oh, I studied hard for that test! I really did. As a freshman, I was an all-A student—mainly because I was so scared of being beaten like some of the other failing students. It was kind of like acknowledging a badge of courage for students, and we would never tell our parents. The priests were always considered right, and we just learned to live with it and keep our mouths shut.

On the day of the test, I was prepared. It was a quick test with only ten questions, and we were given a brief time to answer the questions. When time was called, we were required to literally drop our pens or pencils in the slot at the top portion of our wooden desks.

As I was zooming through the questions one at a time, there was one that simply drew a blank and I could not recall the answer. I passed by it momentarily and finished the rest of the questions. I went back to review the unanswered question and still couldn't think of the answer. Just at the exact moment that I remembered the correct answer, Fr. Z announced, "Time!" I had no other choice but to drop my pen on the desk and pass my paper forward immediately. Realizing that I had missed one question, my fate was doomed to not receive 100 percent on the test.

As several days passed, the more scared I became thinking about when the test results would be revealed. How would I stand up to the punishment of not meeting his 100 percent requirement? The day came, and I was really scared. Most of the students who did not get a hundred were physically struck with the rod several times on the arms, hands, or body as they tried to ward off the fiberglass rod. A decision on my part was firmly made to just sit there with my palms down on the desk and not to move or put my arms up in any defense when the punishment commenced.

Fr. Z approached my desk and placed the paper on my desk. He had a higher-pitched voice, and he placed his thumb over the grade as he said, "Al, do you know what you got?"

I said, "Well Father, I know I didn't get a hundred."

He rolled his thumb off my score, and it was a 93 percent on the test (AKA an A). He began to holler at me and remind me that everyone was required to get a hundred on the test! Standing at my side, he took his rod and began to smack my hands that were face down on the desk in front of me. He struck them over and over, and I just sat there with tears rolling down my cheeks, trying to take it like a man. He then moved on to the next boy. I was hurting both emotionally on the inside and physically on the outside. Growing up was no fun on that day.

My hands began to swell up with black and blue welts. I could barely move my hands and was advised by my friends to go to the infirmary at lunchtime. The nursing staff put salve on the welts and wrapped my hands. It took several days for the swelling to go down and for my hands to get back to normal use. That punishment was for getting an A on a test!

Fr. Zdrodowski really did genuinely like me as a student and followed my progress since he also was the principal of the high school. We would have quarterly academic counseling sessions over my remaining years, and he would always encourage me. We were required to purchase our class rings during our junior year. My parents did not have the money to provide me with that ring, and when Fr. Zdrodowski heard that I couldn't afford a ring, he personally purchased the ring for me. I really appreciated it, and I was very grateful for his kindness. I wore my class ring as a definite badge of courage.

In other classes, students feared failing a test since we were all aware of the different sorts of corporal punishments that would result. I needed tough discipline to finally untie me from my mother's apron strings but the process was not happy at all. I would often cry when I was alone, yet I was determined to become a priest—no matter what it took. I did not hate my teachers in any way, and I knew they really cared about the students. Much of this school was like being in a camp dedicated to building camaraderie. It was somewhat like the Marine Corps.

Yes, discipline was the norm at this all-boys' school, and we had lots of it. I was getting tougher by the day. During my freshman year, we ate all our meals in the refectory. Our meals were prepared and served by Felician nuns who were housed on campus. The food was often plain, but once a week, we had a special dish.

On Sunday mornings, after our six to eight o'clock Solemn High Mass, which was conducted in three languages (Polish, Latin, and English), the student body would immediately assemble afterward for breakfast in the refectory. We would each get one large, tasty pork sausage with the meal. Sometimes when you stuck a fork into it, the grease would stream out of it, over the table, and occasionally onto your clothing. They would serve four sausages in a family style dish, and each of the four boys at our table would get one.

A bully and a nerdy freshman sat at our table of four. The weak kid was nicknamed "Buffalo" because he had bad breath. The bully would always take Buffalo's sausage and eat both. Week after week, Buffalo went without his sausage, never challenging the bully.

One Sunday morning, I had had enough. When the bully grabbed the dish, I grabbed the dish at the same time. He looked at me with a snarl on his face and asked me what I was doing. I told him that he was not going to take Buffalo's sausage anymore.

He said, "Yeah, what are you gonna do about it?"

I just held the bowl in my hand.

He said, "Meet me behind the gym at one o'clock."

I hollered, "I'll be there!"

Was I insane? I had only wrestled with Jerome during my growing up years at the Co-Op. I may have gotten into a fight here and there, but I really don't recall too many fights with anyone growing up since I was a real mama's boy.

I was so scared that I went to my dorm room and began praying nonstop. I kept telling myself that I wasn't assuredly going to go behind the gym. I knew I would get beaten up. It was the worst feeling inside, but I knew I had to go. I left my dorm room and slowly began to walk to the gym just before one o'clock. I arrived there and waited around there for twenty minutes. Guess who didn't show up. Yep, the bully backed down, and believe me, I was greatly relieved. However, I did think I might get in one or two punches before I fell.

During the remainder of the school year, the bully never opened his mouth again or took someone else's food. Yes, Lord, I was

==beginning to learn to stand on my own two feet—no matter what happened. Righteousness bore its fruit, or in this case, sausage.==

All the freshmen students were required to play intramural basketball, and I really stunk at basketball. I voluntarily joined our intramural hockey program (after Orchard Lake froze over in the winter) and subsequently found myself on crutches two years in a row from a fractured ankle and a sprained foot. I was a reasonably good hockey player and liked playing ice hockey since all the kids at Co-Op grew up playing hockey together after the winter freeze at nearby Red Run Drain.

I signed up for the football team at Orchard Lake and played on the JV football team for two seasons and then the varsity squad for my junior season. Not being the worst player, I was certainly not the best either. Somebody had to be second string. I suffered injuries in football—but not as many as in hockey. I struggled to learn shotput on the track team and played on the varsity golf team. I grew up playing golf around the house with my brother Gary and spent several summers caddying at Red Run Golf Course in Royal Oak (a private club). Hockey and golf were the sports that I excelled in. From the rough-and-tumble sports to the tranquil times of playing golf, my life was taking shape and heading me toward manhood. Sports were vitally significant as I grew out of boyhood.

In my sophomore year, a required academic subject was biology. The class was scheduled for the second hour each day. Fr. Kubik would always call on me first. Thinking back now, I wonder why I did not see this everyday pattern. He would introduce us as "doctors" in a joking way. He would say, "Dr. Novak, come up here in front of the class and tell the other doctors what you learned about the reproductive system of the frog found on pages 45–46."

I had eight classes to prepare for each day, and I really hated biology and basically all the other science classes. Biology was the last homework assignment that I would address, and often run out of time during evening study hall. It was very hard to complete all my homework assignments each day and I often fell short.

After being called forward by Fr. Kubik as a doctor to the front of the class, standing with my back to the blackboard, facing my schoolmates and generally being totally unprepared, I would say, "Well, you see, these two frogs get together, and they smooch one another and blah-blah-blah."

Fr. Kubik would be rolling his eyes and shaking his head. He would say, "Mr. Novak, you are no doctor—you are a peasant! Let me show you what they do with peasants." He would grab my head and smash it back into the blackboard twice. I had a headache after the second hour every day for the entire first semester.

He would say, "Sit down, you miserable peasant. You will be a peasant for the rest of your life! You won't be on the top of the sewer shoveling it in; you will be down in the bottom shoveling it out!"

Laughing now while recalling these events; however, I wasn't laughing then. I was being used as a parody of unpreparedness, and it was quite humorous, excluding the two head bangs into the blackboard. He was making his point about how a lack of diligent study will keep you on the bottom and always looking up.

Fr. Kubik had a very unusual way of grading his class. He would assign us certain pages to study for a test. On the test day, he would give us questions that were on another part of the biology book. Naturally, everyone would fail. Grades came in with marks like twelve, eighteen, nine, or six. All were excessively failing grades, but at the end of the grading period, he would then grade all students on a curve. So, if one had grades of nine, eighteen, six, ten, and fourteen, they would have an average of eleven. He would grade you by the class average, and depending on the class, you could end up with an A or a D. He may have felt sorry for me since I was called upon first every day with some question and would end up with a headache each morning. He never asked me a question throughout the entire second semester, and I received a B for the overall class.

In our dormitory, I roomed with my special friend, Bob Wieczorek. He and I became best friends during my three years at Orchard Lake, and we always roomed together. In our junior year, our room was just down the hall on the second floor from Fr. Kubik's corner apartment. Each of the teaching priests were housed in roomy corner apartments throughout the dormitory building. There were eight hundred boys housed in the main dorm building plus prefects (seminary students assigned as disciplinarians for the students) and the resident priests.

Fr. Kubik was actually a very nice man. On weekends, he would often have evening parties with his friends. When the party would break up around two thirty in the morning hours, he would walk down the hallway and come into our room with several bags of leftover food and desserts. He would wake us up, and Bob and I were so very grateful since our normal school food was mostly second grade army surplus food. Fr. Kubik's leftover party tidbits were always great, and we were very grateful for his thoughtfulness in dropping them off in our room. He also knew what the food tasted like in the refectory, and I think he enjoyed blessing us.

The class instructor I feared the most was Fr. Wlota. He was a giant of a man with a burly, strong, deep voice. He was my geometry teacher during my sophomore year. I always studied geometry first since being very fearful of him. He had a mannerism that scared everyone. He had been an all-star football and basketball player when he was growing up. He was tough as nails and gave off a very harsh persona to his students.

Geometry homework assignments were always purposely and precisely prepared. He, for some unknown reason, would always call upon me when assigning students to the blackboard. He would say, "Row 3 (rolling his r's) and Novak to the blackboard." It didn't matter what row he called, he would always add, "And Novak to the blackboard."

He had just lectured us about the proper placement of our thumbs when drawing a triangle with a string attached to a piece of chalk. He said, "Make sure that your thumb is on the bottom of the drawing."

I was aware of his instruction, but while overviewing the drawing and standing back a little with my hand holding the string up and not down, there I stood with my thumb at the top.

It was too late! He saw me and began to holler at me. I was shaking on the inside as he approached me with a large hardbound geometry book. Before I could blink, he hit me behind the head, knocking me into the blackboard and to the ground while yelling in a rage. Oh yeah, it was Manhood Prep 101 time! All the classes at Orchard Lake were challenging to say the least. Believe me, I never put my thumb on the top again while standing at the blackboard!

Prior to my junior year, we had our first choice of classes to select, and I chose to take intermediate algebra (kind of an easy repeat of first-year stuff) over advanced algebra, which I was qualified to take. Fr. Wlota taught advanced algebra and I chose to avoid his class. I did not learn until later that he treated his advanced students totally different, and that he was well liked as an instructor. I also heard that he hoped I would have selected his advanced class since I was a very good geometry student. I did not know all of this at the time, and I took myself out of the firing line of Fr. Wlota and chose a less stressful class. My motivation was always prompted by the fear of physical punishment.

During my junior year, I played on the varsity football team and the varsity golf team. I liked football and played as best as I could but wasn't first string quality. However, I did get used to physical pain associated with practices, preparation, and games.

Golf was a bit different. Fr. Scrocki was our coach. In my

freshman and sophomore years, I played on the junior varsity golf team. In my junior season, the two best-scoring senior players had graduated the previous year leaving me as the player with the lowest scores and highest seniority on the team. The new varsity golf team consisted of several sophomores, some new freshmen, and me as the highest upperclassman. However, when it came to naming the captain of the team, I was bypassed for one of the freshmen. Later I discovered that Fr. Scrocki was a close friend with the freshman's dad, and this made me extremely angry!

I finished the season with much bitterness in my heart, remaining still the lowest scorer on the team. I called my mom and dad and told them that I wanted to transfer to St. Mary's of Royal Oak—and that I no longer wanted to be a priest. My heart had sunk into deep sadness, and my desire for the priesthood was crushed after being so unfairly treated by Fr. Scrocki. I was no longer interested in pursuing the priesthood as a vocation and completely abandoned the idea.

One of the highlights in my junior year at St. Mary's of Orchard Lake was receiving personal letters from brother Joe. He was serving in the army during that time. One of his posts after boot camp was Fort Knox, Kentucky. He was assigned as a mail clerk in the military since he had previous postal experience as a civilian.

Joe, like our dad, shared a great sense of humor. During my junior year at Orchard Lake, he and I wrote letters back and forth to one another biweekly or at least monthly. They were hilariously funny. I would laugh as he poked fun at me and everything I was doing in football, hockey, academics, and with my friends. He always encouraged me to play football and hockey and be tough and to continue strong in my academics.

He always sent me spending money with each letter, and that was such a blessing since I had very little during those years. I always thanked him for the money. He ended one letter with this:

"PS. Knock it off about the money. Don't say any more about it. When I feel that I can spare some and send it to you, spend it and forget it. The end." He always ended his letters with "Love, Joe." He was a genuine big brother who loved me. Jesus is referred to as the friend who sticks closer than a brother:

> "But there is a friend who sticks closer than a brother." Proverbs 18:24 (ESV)

Thank You, Jesus!

My parents were only able to pay for a total of three semesters at Orchard Lake. When I got my first job out of high school at Ford Motor Company at the Wixom Assembly plant, I paid off the remaining balance of school debt monthly until it was fully paid. The best thing that happened to me during those years, excluding the good education, was growing up and becoming a man!

CHAPTER 4

Hello, Girls!

As a former priesthood student, my thoughts were not supposed to be about the opposite sex. A Roman Catholic priest takes a vow of celibacy when ordained in the Sacrament of Holy Orders. Things all changed for me when celibacy was no longer in my future. My eyes were now opened wider.

Transferring to a new rival high school in one's senior year is quite a challenge. I had to adjust back to living at home with my parents and two brothers and figure out how to get to school from Madison Heights to Royal Oak each day. After my first few weeks there, I met a senior class member who lived near us in Madison Heights. Antone Travnikar drove to school every day in his beat-up old Studebaker car that also had no heater. He agreed to give me a ride every day in exchange for some gas money.

There were days that we had to scrape ice off the inside of the windshield while we were heading to school on some of those winter mornings. His defroster only blew cold air since his heater core was broken. Antone was a kindhearted student who subsequently become a Franciscan brother. Later he was ordained a Franciscan priest. We had many laughs riding to school in his pile of junk. He was a character and was not part of the in crowd at school. He was very nice and always displayed a heart of gold.

My closest friends at my new school were Tom, Vince, and John. These guys liked to have fun, and we sure had lots of it during my senior year. It was one of the best years of my life.

After leaving St. Mary's of Orchard Lake (red and white) and transferring to St. Mary's of Royal Oak (blue and white), my school allegiance also changed. As a transfer student, my new buddies decided to use me for a major student body laugh.

Both of my high schools were zealous rivals in all sports, and the annual football game was played on a Friday night. I had lettered in football and golf at Orchard Lake and had received a varsity jacket. My pals talked me into bringing my red and white coat to school and wearing it to Mass on Friday morning of the big game. The entire student body was required to attend Mass on Friday mornings. The seniors sat in the pews on the left front of the church, the juniors sat on the right side, and the sophomores and freshmen sat behind them.

Tom, Vince, and John were waiting to coach me at the back of the church. I arrived just before Mass began. After all the students were seated in their pews, my instructions were to walk slowly down the center aisle, proudly displaying my red with white leather-sleeved (boldly engraved) Orchard Lake Varsity jacket.

At the precise moment, they pushed me forward and I walked down the center aisle very slowly.

As I moved along, the other students focused on my back: "Orchard Lake Varsity." Thinking to myself, *Was I senseless or what?* What a way to introduce myself to my new student body. I walked all the way to the front row, genuflected, and sat down on the end of the front pew that had been reserved for me.

If eyes could burn, I began to feel some extreme heat. After Mass, other kids came up to me and asked who I was rooting for.

I replied, "St. Mary's, of course." I moved from red and white to blue and white and found my new digs to be entirely happy ones.

Shortly after beginning my senior year, I noticed that there were some very attractive girls in my class. I was naively unaware that many of boys had been going steady with certain girls. I did not know this and remained basically in the dark with the dating game. Not knowing who was on who's going-steady list, I started to ask girls out for dates. I thought that the best place to begin would be with the cheerleaders since they were all cute. As an unknown newcomer, they would all enthusiastically say, "Yes!" After going on some dates with several of the cheerleaders, I was starting to get a reputation around the school.

Some male classmates were getting worried that I was interfering with their steady girlfriend relationships, and they decided to meet me in the hallway. They shared with me that they were going steady with certain girls that I had been asking out. They were trying to be kind and acted a bit sheepish toward me. They did not appear to be bullyish or looking for a fight. By then, thanks to Orchard Lake, I was ready to defend myself if required. They just wanted me to know the facts.

I told them that I appreciated the information and would respect their choices and no longer date any of their going-steady girlfriends. We parted as friends.

I attended as many of the football games as possible but also worked at the A&P grocery store on Friday nights as a bagger to earn some spending money. Everybody was excited and cheered for our home team, and we had lots of spirited fun. I happened to notice a girl at one of the games. Terri-Sue Griffith was sitting in the bleachers with some friends. She was one of those National Honor Society girls, and she was a real knock-out. She always seemed to be hanging with a guy named Dick Wells. I thought they were going steady, so I did not approach her for a date.

I found out that she had been formerly dating a boy named John Tapai throughout high school. They were together but supposedly not going steady since all the nuns frowned upon this practice. John was the president of the class and the captain of the football team. During the previous summer, John and his best friend, Dick Wells, had been swimming in a lake together when John had a sudden cramp. Dick tried to save him but was unable to rescue him, and John had drowned. Terri and Dick were simply together as lamenting partners since they both shared the loss of their friend.

Once I was made aware of this, my attention turned toward Terri. We talked together through one complete football game, and she drove me home in her mom's car. I told her that I loved her. *Wow, that was fast!* I was totally infatuated with her charming ways, her polite personality, and her beautiful looks. Those love words came pouring out of my mouth back then without hesitation and later proved to be correct. I knew right then, after talking with her and riding home together, that she was the right girl for me. It was love at first sight.

I noticed her every day at school and decided to ask her out to the next rec (recreational dance). However, I had previously asked out another cheerleader named Betsy. At the dance, I walked over to Terri and asked her to dance. After holding her in my arms and talking to her, I knew she was my future. I told her that I only wanted to dance with her, but she told me that I needed to go back to Betsy since I brought her to the rec. I told her that I looked forward to seeing her again at school, and we parted for the evening.

I only needed one credit to graduate high school. Carrying eight subjects a year at Orchard Lake pushed me way over the required credits except for one English class. So, during my senior year, I decided to have as much fun as possible since I really didn't need to pass any classes except for English.

I rarely studied and generally carried a C average except for English. I even took a typing class. I really enjoyed the class since Terri was in it—and I could see more of her. Sister Reparata, an elderly nun, was a blast as the typing teacher, and she would often throw erasers at me since I was the class clown. The class was invaluable since future computer keyboards were laid out like manual typewriters. Learning basic typing skills was very helpful throughout my entire life.

Terri and I were also in economics class together. Sister Agnes Leo was our Dominican nun teacher. She was very nice and made the class a lot of fun. I would often raise my hand in class and ask her funny questions.

I raised my hand one day and shouted, "Stir, stir?" That was short for sister.

She responded, "Yes, Al?"

I said, "Did you know that you cannot mail letters to Washington any longer?"

She responded very seriously, "Why not?"

I said loudly enough for the entire class to hear, "He's dead!"

She turned completely red, hid behind a book, and laughed.

I was the class clown, and I loved joking around and making others laugh. All my friends thought I was not very smart when it came to academics. They did not know that I had been a very good student at Orchard Lake and carried mostly A and B grades in all my classes.

Before graduation, our senior class had gathered after receiving our four-year high school grade totals with all the class averages and standings included.

Vince, my good friend spoke up loudly, "Hey, Al, what was your class standing?" He assumed that I was most likely ranked near the very last.

I put my head down and said, "I did ok."

He kept pushing me for an answer, but I kept avoiding it. Vince was intelligent and mostly a B+ student, and I presumed that he was in the upper portion of our class. Vince continued to push me.

I finally said, "Well, Vince, I used to study a lot. I had higher grades at Orchard Lake. I only needed one credit in English to graduate when I transferred here. My final class standing was eleventh out of sixty-four students."

He just stood there in shock. He mumbled, "You must be the second-highest boy in class.

I was just behind Joe Zimmer, and he was a very smart student.

Vince kept shaking his head and saying in jest, "But you're a dummy!"

I kept telling Vince that I used to be smart. We both had a great big laugh.

In economics, we occasionally had to give reports on papers that we wrote. After dating several of the girls in class, I apparently was getting a reputation.

Terri got up to give her report that day. She was so cute, and I just couldn't help staring at her. During her audible report, she glanced up, saw me staring at her, and began to blush. Wow, I thought that this blushingly cute girl possibly liked me. I started to yearn to be with her all the time.

So, we began to date on a regular basis. The nuns were opposed to students "going steady" and would discourage it. Their reasoning was that the girls should date a lot of different boys to find out the differences and seek out the favorable qualities and pursue those for their futures. Their concept was actually accurate, but we all seemed to just pair off as reliable couples. I think the nuns liked me because I had disrupted the going-steady group. Most of the couples did drop their relationships after high school, but a few did marry.

Terri and I were walking on the sidewalk out in front of school one day, and we noticed Sister Agnes Leo approaching us. We stopped to chat with her. She asked me what I wanted to do after graduation. I jokingly told her that I wanted to be a TV repairman. She looked at Terri and said, "Terri, drop him like a hot potato!" We all laughed together as we moved along.

Most of the nuns were very kind and really took an interest in us personally. It was a far cry from the stern treatment I had received at Orchard Lake from the priests—even though they really liked us and cared for us as well.

Terri and I grew much closer throughout our senior year. We participated in many school activities together like our recs, school sporting events, our senior play, and our regular classes, and we began to realize that we were falling in love with one another. I often walked her home from school since she lived about a mile away.

We continued to date after our graduation in 1963, and six months later, I proposed to her. I had a good job at Ford Motor Company's Wixom Assembly Plant and was so deeply in love with her. We were married at St. Mary's of Royal Oak on June 6, 1964. It was a smaller wedding, and we began our lives together at age nineteen. Who today gets married at age nineteen? We were just kids ourselves, but we were in love—or at least completely infatuated with one another. I believe now that love takes time to really mature, and then it becomes the foundation of a long-lasting relationship.

I always shared, during wedding ceremonies or marriage counseling sessions, that love is the foundation of a lasting marriage. I concluded that there were three Cs of a successful marriage: Commitment, Communication, and Christ. Commitment is referring to the vows made to God, to spouse, and to others. Communication basically challenges the marriage partners to keep talking to one another. And lastly, Christ needs to be the center of your life and marriage.

Terri and I have now been married for fifty-seven years. I report to you that it does work! It is not a piece of cake, but it is so worth it in the long run to have a loving, faithful companion and friend for life and to avoid the pitfalls of loneliness. Christ made all the difference in our marriage.

CHAPTER 5

Honeymoon Nightmare

We planned out our honeymoon to travel by car all the way out to the East Coast and then drive up into Maine. Our destination was to stop for a few days in Niagara Falls on the way back home to Royal Oak. I had saved up money working at Ford Motor Company, and our wedding gifts totaled eight hundred dollars and a new set of Samsonite luggage. That was quite a bit of money back then and would provide a more comfortable style to our honeymoon travels.

We left late in the afternoon after my car wouldn't start. I reconnected the loose distributor cap that my new brother-in-law, Larry, had disconnected as a prank to delay our departure. We were traveling to the Ohio Turnpike and then eastbound to our first night stay at the Holiday Inn in Elyria-Loraine, Ohio.

The following morning, I pulled up my 1963, two-door hardtop Chevy, Impala (azure-aqua color) with six coats of wax on it, in front of our hotel. I placed our brand-new four-piece set of matching luggage that we had received from Terri's mom as a wedding gift in the trunk. We ate breakfast and glanced out at our car. The sunshine bounced off the car making it appear like it was radiating some heavenly glow. We had visions of paradise as we looked forward to our next two weeks of honeymoon life. I remember thinking to myself that *I must be in heaven!* I don't ever recall being or feeling happier than at that precise moment. I imagined it was a glimpse of what paradise might be like in the future—pure total euphoric ecstasy—and we were there!

We headed east on the Ohio Turnpike that connected us to the Pennsylvania Turnpike. I had our hotel teletype (google it if you do not know what a teletype is) and make a room reservation for the following night at the Holiday Inn in Altoona, Pennsylvania. I also requested a room with a view.

Around two thirty in the afternoon, we found ourselves in stop-and-go traffic congestion on the turnpike. Our honeymoon happened to take place during the 1964 New York World's Fair, and there were miles of very heavy traffic. The Pennsylvania Turnpike was quite narrow at that time; there was an occasional place to pull off the roadway, but most of the time, we were driving right next to a mountainside or very close to the center guardrail. A vehicle in the left lane about five hundred feet ahead of us slowed down and stopped as it waited for a chance to pull into the over-crowded right-hand lane. All the vehicles ahead of us began to slam on their brakes to avoid colliding with the vehicles that were stopping ahead of them, thus creating a five-car chain reaction accident behind them.

Terri and I were the third of the five cars, and I managed to successfully stop, just inches from touching the center guardrail. I looked in my rearview mirror and could see a car bearing down on us. The woman driver had panicked and inadvertently pressed down on the accelerator, thinking it was the brake. She struck us in the rear at about forty-five miles per hour and pushed our car simultaneously forward into the guardrail and into car ahead of us.

She was driving a full-sized brand-new Cadillac, and it resulted in a major collision impact.

Just prior to the impact, I reached my right arm out to block Terri from going forward into the windshield. We did not have seat belts available at that time. The impact caused both of us to lose our sunglasses later finding mine on the back seat window deck. The right front of our car was pushed forward into the vehicle ahead of us and our trunk was caved in—with all our new luggage inside.

We were all stopped in the left lane of traffic. I was able to chug our car over to the shoulder since everyone was either pushed or towed over to the side. There must have been over fifty miles of backed-up traffic, and it took us quite some time to remove all the vehicles from the roadway.

After the Pennsylvania State Police arrived, each driver was interviewed, and all the accident reports were taken. The tow truck driver, after checking my car, said that it appeared that my distributor cap was cracked apart since the engine had shifted forward and bounced back, snapping it in half. The distributor cap was situated on the back of the engine near the firewall. He just happened to have one in his truck, and after replacing it and pulling our front fender free from the wheel, we were able to continue our drive. We finished at the scene, and we decided to wait until we got to Altoona to pry open the trunk.

Once we were on our way, a torrential rain began to fall. The rain was so intense our wipers could not keep up with it at full speed, reducing our travel to thirty miles per hour. Our room was only reserved until six o'clock, and we were still not very close to our destination.

I found an exit off the turnpike and located a phone booth (something that one might see in an old-time movie). Standing inside the phone booth, I placed the needed coins into the pay phone slot as raindrops were leaking from the top of the booth and landing directly on top of my head. I was able to contact the hotel in Altoona and confirm our stay until nine o'clock since almost everything was fully booked along our route.

After getting back on the road, my neck stiffened up. Unknowingly I had suffered a whiplash during the accident and could barely turn my neck. Terri and I were extremely hungry from not eating all day, and we passed by several hot dog places while looking for our hotel as we arrived in Altoona. The rain had not let up at all. The ascending driveway entrance to the Holiday Inn was like a river, and I felt like I was traveling uphill in a boat as we splashed forward to our destination.

We arrived at 9:05 p.m., and I registered at the inn. I asked if their restaurant was still open and of course it had closed at nine. We jumped back into the car and drove back to the first hot dog stand we came to. I stood under a tiny little awning and ordered our food as huge raindrops dripped down my neck.

I requested six hot dogs and hamburgers, fries, and an assortment of other junk food. We stopped at a small drugstore that was still open, and Terri went in and purchased some Ben-Gay for my stiff neck. We were famished at that point, and our bodies were sore and hurting from being tossed about during the accident. We were also extremely exhausted from the hard traveling conditions that we had just experienced en route to our hotel.

We returned with the bags of food to our room and parked in front of our reserved space. I pried open our trunk and was so grateful that there had been no significant damage to the luggage. I placed our luggage in our room, and we began to eat hurriedly to satisfy our ravenous appetites. I noticed an odd smell to the hot dogs, but I ate them anyway. Terri chose a hamburger. I scoured down one after another, chomping on fries in between.

Still soaking wet from the rains, we decided to take showers and put on some dry clothes. In the shower, my neck tightened up fully from the whiplash. After my shower, I asked Terri to put some Ben-Gay on my neck. Being a loving and concerned new wife and formerly in the future nurse's club in high school, she applied an exceptionally hot towel to my neck for a little while and then spread a palmful of the Ben-Gay all over my neck. Thinking that it might not be enough, she also applied a second layer.

Finally falling asleep on my back, I felt the heat from the Ben-Gay begin to radiate into my neck. Within a short time, my stomach began growling and making gurgling sounds as I began to feel queasy and sick to my stomach. I jumped out of bed, rushed over to the toilet, and began to vomit. A sudden awareness surfaced that I was suffering from food poisoning from the bad-tasting hot dogs and remained woozy for several hours. After a short time had passed, I was finally able to drift off to sleep.

After sleeping for a little while, I opened my terror-filled eyes and thought somebody was holding a blowtorch on my neck. The burning sensation generated from the Ben-Gay was so intense that I jumped out of bed, ran into the shower, turned on the ice-cold water, and put my neck under the flow. I thought to myself, *This morning at eleven o'clock, I was looking at my beautiful wife sitting across the breakfast table from me and my sparkling new car with the sunshine bouncing off the six coats of wax, knowing that this was the very first day of our honeymoon and that must be heaven!*

Less than fifteen hours later, it seemed like I had been drop-kicked out of heaven and was living in some demonic nightmare. Somehow, I managed to make it through the night and amazingly discovered that my neck seemed much better and surprisingly moveable. The Ben-Gay had worked some form of miracle in my whiplashed neck. I pulled open the sun-laden curtains in our room to see the panorama of our requested "room with a view," and there was some type of construction going on in the back of the hotel. A giant hill of fresh dirt was totally blocking any view.

The pangs of disappointment continued to press upon us, but we decided to drive back to the Holiday Inn in Elyria-Loraine, Ohio, and spend a few days there to determine a plan for the remaining days of our honeymoon. After arriving back in Ohio, we parked our damaged vehicle way in the back lot out of view to forget our recent experiences.

A few days later, we decided to return to Michigan, get our car repaired, and then go somewhere in Michigan for the remainder of our honeymoon. We did exactly that and began our new life together. I thought, *If we could weather our rough start, maybe we could keep our commitments to a lifetime of being together.* We have been together as husband and wife since that day in 1964. We thank God since the road ahead of us had many ruts and potholes. We avoided some and sank into others, but by God's grace, we continued along our road together.

CHAPTER 6

A Cop's Life

Adjusting to the life of a full-time police officer and rotating shifts each month was difficult. Most people will never see or experience the terrible life experiences that law enforcement officers observe almost daily. In fact, most people only get a little glimpse of real life on TV, cop documentaries, news features, or stories of real-life incidents. They might occasionally read stories in the newspaper about some of these incidents. Most people thankfully never experience life in the raw. Not so with cops. Their lives are touched by heart-wrenching real-life situations that are lived out right in front of them. It is very difficult to deal with these hard facts of life, and most officers must find a source of strength somewhere. They personally need to find some peace in their life; after all, they are one hundred percent human beings.

There are complete stories behind the following incidents that remain to this day in my memory bank. I recall holding a two-year-old baby boy who had been beaten to death by his parents. I pulled another little boy out of the bottom of a pool in a drowning accident while the mother was hysterically screaming for me to save her child; sadly, it was too late. Another young woman had taken rat poison and was found on her garage floor with her face half eaten away. A thirteen-year-old boy had taken a .22 caliber rifle and placed it to his chest and was found dead in a mound of garbage in the dining room of his house. I was called to a scene of an injury accident on a Sunday morning. Upon arrival, looking into the back seat of one of the vehicles, I could not distinguish whose arm belonged to whose body and whose head belong to which body. In that accident, two elderly parents died, and a twenty-three-year-old daughter became a paraplegic for the rest of her life.

In a family dispute, I arrived to discover a woman pointing to the bedroom and screaming, "He's in there, Officer!"

He was in there, all right. Half of his brains had been scattered on the wall. He had taken a shotgun and ended his marriage and his life. A young girl was found in a motel room lying on a bed with a needle stuck in her arm and a half-smile on her face; she had surrendered to death with her last jab of heroin.

I often saw the utter waste of precious life in our so-called 1967 All-American City of eighty-five thousand people, which was just a few miles north of Detroit. I could go on and on with real-life stories during those seventeen years, but I think you get the picture. Police officers see things that most people do not see or really want to see. How does a cop handle these experiences emotionally?

I really didn't know how to handle these feelings. Oh, during the many hours of police training, we were taught to develop good exercise habits, watch our diets, practice self-meditation, and other secular and Freudian mumbo-jumbo. Coping with all these tragedies was not easy, and the training preparations fell short in meeting our psychological needs.

After joining the police force in 1966, I was assigned to a shift of about twenty-five uniformed officers plus the command staff.

I considered myself to be a Christian by virtue of my religious background, but I was not born-again into the spiritual realm yet. I wanted to fit in with my fellow officers since they were a very close-knit and fraternal group.

The guys would meet several times a month to play cards and have a few beers. They asked me to join in, and I obliged. Everyone wants to be accepted by their peers, and I was no different. I was not a drinker back then, but as I joined in with my peers, one beer led to another. Overtime I became dependent upon alcohol as my coping mechanism. Progressive insobriety is how I dealt with my real-life psychological encounters for about ten years.

When the afternoon shift would end, I would head for the local bar and bathe my perplexing concerns in alcohol. There was some temporary appeasement, but the very next day, it would start all over again. Life seemed a bit fuzzier than the day before with newly added and compounded family problems. Those were the years that I struggled with some of my greatest inner confrontational issues, and I seemed to be losing ground daily.

Terri and I began to grow apart. She told me that she and the kids would pray and light candles at church for me. We had two children under five and one on the way before my fifth year of police work. Terri did not have much time at the end of her busy day for selfish me. The days that I would come home after work, she was busy attending to the kids. I also wrestled with parental skills since most of my childhood days were spent as a loner and an introvert. I know that my dad loved me, but he never said those words to me. Rotating shifts each month created another problem in our family life—along with working on weekends and just about every holiday.

During that time, listening friendships were developed at the local pub. My brother officers and bar friends substituted as my wife during those years. I worked part-time jobs to keep up with my bar tabs and extracurricular social activities like gambling trips to Vegas and the Bahamas. A store detective, guard jobs, short-order cook, building houses, and even owning a small country variety store took many hours away from my home life and lessened my connectivity as a husband and father.

My street image acquainted me as a "tough but fair" cop who performed his duties well. My fellow officers thought favorably of me, and I got along rather well with most of them. My Catholic religious upbringing had taught me to treat others like I would like to be treated, and my police duties were usually performed with that effort in mind.

It was not uncommon even after issuing a traffic citation to a violator, I would get a thank you from the driver. They certainly weren't thanking me for writing them a ticket; they were thanking me for treating them with respect as a person and citizen. I always attempted to treat each person the same way that I would like to be treated if I were stopped for a traffic violation. Some people would write letters to our chief to commend my respectful attitude toward them. As a career officer, I found great satisfaction in policework along with what I thought were reasonably good wages and benefits. Overall, I was enjoying my life—the good times and the challenging times together—but I was craving the good times more often.

On a midnight shift, as a rookie, I was assigned to ride with an officer named Fred Smith. We had a north end beat, and Officer Fred was a prideful but thorough police officer in his duties. He was my senior officer, and I was taught to keep my mouth shut and just learn the ropes.

We received a call to a house on the north end that an assailant had shot and killed a person in Berkley, a borderline city of ours, drove to his home in Royal Oak, and barricaded himself inside. He was armed with a .30-06 caliber rifle with a scope and announced that he would not be taken alive. This all began after midnight when the most challenging police work generally occurs. All the available cars and officers had responded and positioned themselves around the house with everyone hiding behind cars, bushes, and poles. At that time, we did not carry shotguns or high-powered rifles in our squad cars.

Officer Fred Smith and I were ordered to return to our police headquarters and gather up the rifles and shotguns and ammunition from our armory, return to the scene, and distribute the firearms to the officers surrounding the house.

Arriving back on the scene, my instructions were to load and hand-deliver the weapons and ammunition. Following orders, I concealed myself as much as possible and carried rifles and shotguns under both arms and distributed them to the officers. I would sneak from bush to pole to car, staying as hidden as possible.

After completing my assignment, we waited. Our command officers tried to communicate with the suspect. They offered him options, but he refused and continued his threats to kill any officer he saw. He was a very angry person and was severely intoxicated. I guess we all knew that time was on our side as we waited him out. We knew that he would eventually give in to sleep.

At four thirty in the morning, our lieutenant on the scene told us to charge the house and kick in the front door. He was sleeping on the couch, and the high-powered rifle was on his chest. He was arrested, and we all vacated the scene. Thanks be to God—no one was hurt at that scene.

The next day, Detective Gliwa came into our squad room during lineup. He asked, "Who was the officer passing out the shotguns and rifles at the scene of the barricaded gunman last night?"

Several of the officers pointed to me and told him that it was Novak.

I nodded my head in agreement.

Detective Gliwa spoke up and said that the suspect wanted me to know that he had me in the "crosshairs" of his scope twice but failed to pull the trigger. He said that he was squeezing off both times but for some reason held his fire. This was before bulletproof vests were even available; however, a vest would not have stopped a .30-06 bullet. At that time, I really didn't think too much about the situation. I just considered it part of my duty as a police officer; taking risks just came with the job.

Thirty-five years later, while up north hunting deer, I was looking down a powerline trail and observed a large doe walk into the clearing. I had a doe permit and was hunting with a high-powered .308 rifle with a scope. As I looked at the deer through the crosshairs of my scope, a sudden chill went up and down my spine. In an instant flash back, I was reminded of that precise moment when that murder suspect had me in the crosshairs of his scope. An up-to-date shockwave was sent to my memory bank. I looked at that deer in the crosshairs of my scope and realized that God had saved me from certain death that day. It really was a very special moment, some twenty plus years later, as I began praising the Lord for saving my life. I would have died in my sin and ultimately been tossed into the lake of fire that is forewarned in the scriptures. Please think about the following question: Are you presently living in your sin? Do you really want forgiveness? Some good news is that the blood of Jesus can take away all your sin. This does require a sincere act of faith and trust in Him. Jesus Christ is truly the answer!

Another domestic incident that toyed with my mental psyche was the family troubles of Mr. and Mrs. Beyer. They were a deep southern speaking couple who were involved in continuous and repeat domestic troubles. Many such times we would get a dispatch to their house in response to a "family fight." It was usually a neighbor who called.

Mrs. Beyer would always be beaten up and found bleeding, and Mr. Beyer would be drunker than a skunk. That was years before any domestic protection laws had been enacted. We would generally try to get one of them to leave for the night for the sake of peace. Sometimes she would leave. If Mr. Beyer was too drunk to move or unconscious, she would just stay. When he would sober up, they would just continue living out their troubled lives together. After all, he was the provider and breadwinner and had a good job in the auto factory.

Every time we were called to that scene, Mrs. Beyer in her southern drawl would say, "One of these days, I'm a gonna get him!" We heard these same threats for several years repeatedly.

One day, we received a call from the neighbor that the Beyers were at it again—and that there was an unusual smell coming from the house. When we walked in, Mrs. Beyer was standing at the stove. She was humming a tune to herself and smiling. When she saw us, she shouted, "I finally got him" as she was stirring some meat in her skillet.

I said, "Well, where is he?"

She pointed to the closet just off the kitchen. We opened the door and found him. There was blood all over his cut-opened chest, and he was dead.

She smiled and said, "He had a mean heart! I told you I would get him someday." She had stabbed him to death with a kitchen knife after he tried to beat her up again. She cut out his "mean old heart" and decided to fry it in the cast iron skillet. As she stirred the pan, she kept saying, "He had a mean heart!"

That was the final family fight call to the Beyer's residence. She was committed for a mental evaluation, and his body was transported to the morgue. These are some of the real-life situations that police officers observe daily and must find a way to psychologically cope with and manage in their own lives. How do you do that as a police officer—and more importantly as a human being?

CHAPTER 7

God, Please Help Me!

After ten years of policework, things changed drastically. I had been injured on duty while arresting a drunk out on Woodward Avenue during a traffic stop. I had succumbed to a pinched nerve in my lower back. The three most common problems with career police officers are: eye problems from constant strain, especially at night, back troubles from too much sitting in cars, and hemorrhoids.

Sciatic nerve pain traveled down my left leg that generated from a pinched nerve in my lower back. Eventually I was admitted into William Beaumont Hospital under the care of an orthopedic surgeon. I had spent many hours at the hospital taking police reports from victims over the past ten years. They placed me in a room with a man that I recognized was near death. He was an elderly man, and I just knew that he was dying. I could hear him at night with what I called the death rattle, which often emanated from people who were very close to the end of life. My desire was to help this man, but I could only lie there with intense sciatic nerve pain pulsating down my leg. My face was covered with cold sweat as I agonized for hours over both situations.

As it was with soldiers facing a pending battle, I cried out to God. "Oh, God! Please help me!" Somehow, I believe He heard my sincere cry. The elderly man survived the night, and the next morning, he was sent home. It was the policy of the hospital to allow terminal patients to return home and die in their comfortable surroundings. Terminal patients now have hospice to assist with comfort care until the end.

The hospital custodians straightened up the room immediately after he was released. A fresh bed was made, and the curtain was opened wide so I could see the sun shining through the window. My spasms had eased up a little from the Tylenol that I had been given. I was fitted into a pelvic traction apparatus, and weights were placed on the end of the bed. Stretching was then applied to my lower pelvic area to relieve the pain and pressure. This was a natural way to get blood flowing to the pinched area of the back. We were hopeful that this would work under the supervision of my doctor and only time would tell.

CHAPTER 8

God Sends Help

S hortly after noon, my next roommate arrived. Ron was a Royal Oak schoolteacher. We talked about our medical conditions. I found out that Ron was about to undergo surgery for a fragmented disk in his lower back.

We talked about sports, TV, our families, and our occupations. Ron was very athletic and was a genuine outdoorsman. He also was an avid tennis player. Our conversations eventually led to religion. Ron asked if I went to church.

I told him that I was a Catholic and had been all my life.

He told me that he was a "born-again Christian."

I said, "Heh, that's great! Everybody should be a born-again Christian." I had no idea what a born-again Christian was, but I was happy for him.

When we talked about his upcoming surgical procedure, Ron said, "Al, I am trusting in the Lord!"

I told him I thought it might be better if he trusted in his neurosurgeon because it was the surgeon who wielded the scalpel in his hand.

"No," Ron said. "I am sure, Al, that God will take charge over the surgery, and I can trust completely in Him."

Ron was trusting in God, and Ron's wife shared the same confession with me. Ron's pastor came for a visit and assured me that they were all trusting in God for Ron's recovery and that his church family was praying for him. I was quite impressed with their faith in God. I sensed that it was not the normal pie-in-the-sky faith encounter that I had experienced throughout religion. They all seemed to be at peace about the whole situation, which I found very amazing.

I began to develop a closer-knit relationship with Ron as our time together continued, and I became very concerned for him as my roommate and friend. I was set up in pelvic traction for the duration of my hospital stay and was receiving no medication at all. The nurses were very generous when fellow police officers and friends would visit with me and bring me bottles of rum, mix, and other alcoholic beverages. The cabinet next to my hospital bed became a well-stocked liquor cabinet for my visitors and me to enjoy. Even the nurses—ignored the hospital policies with me being a cop—brought me lots of ice upon request. Most of my visitors were police officers or friends with whom I associated during my off-duty hours. I didn't hang out with servile people, but my friends were professional people like dentists, lawyers, store owners, restaurant and cocktail lounge owners, prominent businessmen, and police officers.

A good friend of mine was a local businessman, and he thought it would be neat to do a promo by having a couple of "Playboy bunnies" pay me a visit. Their visit was intended to lift the spirits of one of Royal Oak's finest as he was confined to a hospital bed along with promoting a nearby Detroit Playboy Club. The story and photo made the front page of the *Daily Tribune*. I had a self-conscious grin as I was flanked by two beautiful bunnies on each side of the bed. *Man, this is living,* I thought.

Ron graciously tolerated the frivolities transpiring from my side of the room. He would smile my way from time to time without any condemning looks. He later shared with me that he was a deacon in his church. He said that he was playing with his little baby near the bottom of his stairway when he accidently slid down three steps. That was when the disk in his lower back had fragmented. I thought, *I wonder why Ron isn't angry at God? I sure would be! It's one thing to be out living a sinful life and get hurt—maybe as a punishment from God—but to be at home, living a righteous life and being a good daddy and a family man, and receive a punishment from God?*

I would have shaken my fist at God and angrily asked, "Why are you doing this to me?" That's what Job asked. I later learned that God does not do such things at all, but Satan (a.k.a. the devil) deliberately and intentionally desires to kill, steal, and destroy us. Ron never spoke a word against God. His only comments were to reassure me that God would take care of him. I recognized this as a true walk of faith, and Ron's faith proved accurate.

His delicate neurosurgery was a complete success, and his recovery was very swift. On Christmas Eve 1974, after twelve days together in the hospital, we were both released. Ron was going home to recuperate, and I was released to go home because it was Christmas Eve. My wife borrowed a hospital bed, and they set up pelvic traction for me there. I was eager to be home for Christmas.

As Ron and I were waiting to be released, he reached his hand out to shake my hand. As we shook hands, Ron said, "Al, I just want to tell you that I love you."

I gulped, stammered, and choked as the return response came from my lips. I cleared my throat and said, "I ... I love you too, Ron." My thoughts may have been revealed in my blushing face. At the time, it was hard saying those words even to my wife. We had gone through some very rough years together with several separations and a near divorce. I couldn't even say those words to our three children since I had become very reclusive and a self-centered parent.

Desires for self-medicating alcohol kept me apart from my family, and I spent most of my free hours with my bar friends. I was so egocentric that I couldn't really love anyone other than myself at that juncture of my life. I thought, *I sure hope my fellow police officers never find out that I told another man that I loved him. They would most likely begin to wonder about me!* I kept this all to myself, but Ron's life and his revealed faith and trust in God never left my thoughts.

CHAPTER 9

Acupuncture

I went home and remained in pelvic traction for several more weeks. I finally was released back to work and assigned to light desk duty and radio dispatch. Gradually, my injury improved, and I subsequently went back on the road. It wasn't too long afterwards that the pain returned with greater intensity.

I heard about some state certified medical doctors who treated patients with acupuncture. They were in Brighton, MI and people came from all over the world for their treatments. They were both Chinese. One of the workers at the Department of Public Works, Charlie, whose job was to maintain the squad cars, told me his acupuncture story. He said that he had three pinched nerves in his neck and was so disabled that he could only walk doubled over. He tried all kinds of treatments and finally submitted to the acupuncture treatments. Charlie now walked completely straight backed and had no pain whatsoever. He said, "Al, I guess you should know this. These doctors have Bible verses hanging on the waiting room walls of their clinic, and they personally pray over patients before they began the treatments."

I laughed and said, "Well, Charlie, I could use all the prayers I can get because the place I am headed for will require a very big air conditioner."

We both chuckled, and I took down the information. I called and scheduled an appointment for the next week. I thought, *What do I have to lose?*

The muscle spasms continued to worsen. I was in great pain most of the time. I had become immune to the Darvon medication that my doctor had prescribed for pain. After a month of straight use, I finally took myself off the Darvon for fear of becoming addicted. My cop mentality concluded that all drug addicts really belonged behind bars. I certainly did not want to be hooked on drugs. The sciatic nerve pain had grown in intensity, and it often seemed as though someone was going up and down my right leg with a blowtorch. I was now constantly in pain.

Terri drove me to the acupuncture clinic in Brighton, which was about an hour away from our Ortonville home. When we arrived, I struggled to get out of the car. The waiting room was filled with people from all over the United States. I did not realize how well-known these two doctors were. I also noticed the Bible verses hanging on the walls in the waiting room. I read them as best I could, but the pain robbed my concentration.

When I was finally called to go in, they escorted me to a room with ten beds or so. I was told to remove my shirt and lie face down. I waited about ten minutes for the doctor to arrive. Dr. Stella K. Weng Cheng was short-statured and looked certifiably Chinese. She said with an accent, "How you doin', Meester Novak! I am Dr. Stella Weng Cheng. Please tell me what is wrong with you."

I told her about my injury and the sciatic nerve pain that was getting progressively worse.

She told me that I needed to understand that Chinese acupuncture was only a tool in God's hand and that she and her husband, Dr. Weng Cheng, believed that God did the healing. She asked me if she could pray over me before they began the treatment.

I said, "Sure, why not!"

She and her husband and another nurse stood over me, placed their hands on my back, and began to pray. They asked God to heal me in their prayers and recognized Him as the healer. They concluded their prayer by saying, "In the name of Jesus, we pray. Amen."

Dr. Stella, being very short, had to reach up over my back to put seventeen needles down my spinal column. She asked what I did for a living, and I told her I was a police officer. As she began with a brief demonstration, she placed one long, thin needle in the fatty area between my left index finger and thumb.

I was lying on my stomach, and I was amazed that the needle sticking in me really didn't seem to hurt at all.

She started inserting the acupuncture needles down my back. Every time she would insert a needle, I would flinch a little. The needles going in didn't bother me, but my sensitivity to any touch was very high since I had so many spasms up and down my back. I would jump slightly each time she placed a needle into my body.

She finally said, "What's wrong with you?"

I said, "It hurts."

She said, "Aw, you big *poleeseman*. It no hurt you. You big *poleeseman*." She chuckled slightly, and I couldn't tell whether she was kidding. She kept putting the needles in my back—all seventeen of them—and I must have jumped seventeen times. She kept saying, "You no hurt, you big *poleeseman*."

She then attached a red positive lead to the top needle nearest my neck and a black negative lead to the needle farthest down my back. The leads were attached to an electronic machine that began to send a pulsating current down my back. The pulsating throbs lasted for about fifteen or twenty minutes. When I was through, she stopped the machine, removed all the needles, and told me that I was finished for the day. I was told to come back for another treatment in a couple days.

I left the office that day feeling slightly different, but still in pain. I received several more treatments for the next month. The results were all about the same—until I received the fourth treatment.

Dr. Weng Cheng, Dr. Stella's husband, told me that they were now going to try the "old ancient Chinese acupuncture." Now this was different. They inserted the seventeen needles again, but they were longer in size and had a sheathing on the end. Each needle was spun between his fingers until it felt warm to hot at each insertion point.

When the treatment was completed, I got up from the table very slowly. I knew something had happened because for the first time I felt no pain at all.

It was like being in some form of euphoric state as Terri assisted me back to the car. I thought it was best not to drive since everything seemed weird or hazy. There seemed to be a mist over my eyes wherever I looked. I felt lightheaded and exhilarated, and yet the pain was gone. The cloudiness drifted away after a few hours, and the pain did not return. It was the first time I had been free of pain in a year a half without any pain medication.

I was extremely excited and overjoyed with the results. *The Chinese God had been good to me,* I thought. I told Terri to pack our suitcases and prepare the kids because we needed a vacation to Florida deciding to take the family to Disney World.

The kids were very excited as we drove south on I-75, and I was thrilled to be driving my car without any pain. We stayed overnight in Kentucky, and as we drove through Georgia the next day, I started to feel pain down my leg again. The acupuncture had worked for a few days, but it didn't last. I subsequently became discouraged as the pain returned.

We spent the week in Florida and took the kids to Disney World and to some other theme parks. My demeanor changed negatively since the pain had returned, and my hope was beginning to diminish. It grew steadily worse and became unbearable at times during that week. I knew I would have to search further medically when we got back to Michigan. I thought that this may require surgery, like my former hospital roommate Ron had undergone, as the final solution. I had not personally met up with Jesus yet, and I knew nothing of God's deep care, concern, and love for me. My heart needed to be awakened to His presence and availability, but I did not know it yet.

CHAPTER 10

The Problems Increase

After a difficult drive home from Florida, an appointment was scheduled with a neurosurgeon. Following an initial examination, I was admitted back into Beaumont Hospital for some new tests. This time, the atmosphere was not jovial, and it was time to do whatever was necessary to find some pain relief. My doctor did some routine and neurological tests, including blood, urine, stool, x-rays, and a myelogram. The myelogram procedure was done in the operating room.

The morning of the myelogram, I was given an injection to relax me. I was then taken into the operating room and placed on an x-ray table. While on my stomach, the doctor had to insert a long needle into my spine to remove all my spinal fluid. This test replaced my spinal fluid with a contrast dye that would be visible during the x-rays of my back. This would permit them to see clearly where the damaged or pinched nerve was located.

As the doctor began the procedure the large needle inadvertently penetrated a central nerve in the middle of my spinal column. When this occurred, even under sedation, I cried out in anguish. My body pushed upward with intense pain that lifted me off the table. I know this must have startled the doctor and nurses. I experienced what I thought to be a taste of the Spanish Inquisition. I would have confessed to anything at that point. "Yes, I did it, stop!"

They continued with the myelogram and reinserted the needle. The doctor drew out my spinal fluid and replaced it with the contrast dye. The x-rays were taken as they moved the table up and down with my head and feet exchanging locations. The contrast die was moving through my spinal column, giving them a look at my problem. Their observations were noted, and my spinal fluids and dye were re-exchanged, and I was moved to the recovery room.

I was instructed not to move my head at all for twenty-four hours. Otherwise, I would have severe headaches from the spinal fluid exchange. The next morning, a battery of interns arrived in my room to review my case. They unwittingly began to move my legs and body around checking things out, since I was unable to move them under my own power. I experienced some form of paralysis after the myelogram and had little mobility below my neck and continued suffering with the sciatic leg pain. After the interns left, my head began to pound with a severe headache. A spinal headache, which they warned me would happen if I lifted my head, had begun. I always wondered why the interns were not aware that they were not to move me for twenty-four hours. The headaches persisted for several days, and all they could give me was Tylenol.

After the headaches diminished, I continued to notice little mobility below my neck. I could move my arms, neck, and head, but that was about it. My neurosurgeon came to visit and told me that they had located the injury's precise location, but it was inoperable.

He conferred with specialists in California about my case, and if I underwent surgery, the chances of success were about 20 percent. Not very good odds, but after all the previous medical treatments, I was ready to go for it. I told him to do the surgery.

He told me that he decided to release me to go home and set up pelvic traction again.

I asked him if I was ever going to get out of bed again.

As he was backing out of my room, he said, "Well, Mr. Novak, I'm not sure. Come and see me in a month or so."

I felt completely hopeless at that point. This doctor was the best neurosurgeon at Beaumont Hospital, and he gave me no real hope of recovery. As a matter of fact, I was in a worse condition, and most of my lower body was now paralyzed. The thought began to enter my mind that there was a way out—and I knew how to do it.

CHAPTER 11

God Sends an Angel?

At home, I began to plan my demise since I did not want to remain a vegetable for the rest of my life in a hospital bed. My mind raced as I languished in a continual pity party for Al Novak. There were no more reasons needed to end it all so the decision was formulated. I decided to do it.

As a police officer, I was often dispatched to the scenes of suicides. I had observed people who killed themselves using many ways: shotgun to the head, hanging themselves with a rope, taking rat poison, overdosing on drugs, drinking paint stripper, bullet through the heart, slitting of the wrists, suffocating themselves, carbon monoxide poisoning, freezing to death, drownings, and the list went on and on.

Recalling one incident of an elderly man who called the police from a phone booth and informed us that he was going to kill himself. After talking at length with this man at the scene and locating a loaded shotgun in the bushes near the phone booth, we tried to talk him out of it for several hours. I would have to say that of all the people I met who had identified sufficient reasons to end it all, this man really did have some perceived valid reasons. We were able to dissuade him from killing himself that night. He also chose a very messy way to end his life with a shotgun. My decision was to end it fast and use my service revolver with one bullet to my head.

A few days later, Terri had gone shopping while the kids were at school. We were living in a nice house that I had built in Ortonville with the help of my family, relatives, and friends several years earlier. The hospital bed was set up in the family room with the pelvic traction apparatus. I removed the traction from my waist, rolled to the edge of the bed, and fell to the floor with a thud.

My arms and neck were movable as I struggled to drag my body down the hallway toward our bedroom, where my service revolver was located. As I got halfway down the hallway, there was a knock on the front door. I hollered, "Well, whoever it is, come in!"

A man in a suit identified himself only as John from the workmen's comp program. He told me that he had been sent out by the city to update my medical status.

I asked if he could help me get back into my bed, and he did.

I shared all the medical treatments I had received in the past two years, including orthopedic, acupuncture, and neurosurgical procedures. Thinking of my present-day situation, I began to cry. I wept and sobbed for nearly twenty minutes. I reflected on the fact that if John had arrived just five minutes later, he would have found the corpse of Al Novak. He didn't know that, and he seemed like a very compassionate fellow as he patiently allowed me to cry it out.

After gaining my composure John said, "Well, Al, you have tried all the conventional medical treatments—how about the unconventional?"

I said, "Like what?"

...id, "Well, how about a chiropractor?"

...d him that I didn't think a chiropractor could really help ...e I had received all my previous diagnosis and treatments from the highest rated medical professionals.

He said, "Well, Al, what have you got to lose?"

He left after our conversation, not knowing—or maybe really knowing—that he had given me a glimmer of hope. It was just enough hope to keep me from climbing out of my hospital bed, crawling to our bedroom, and killing myself with my service revolver.

The next day, I called and scheduled an appointment with a chiropractic clinic in Royal Oak.

In the 1970s, chiropractors were allowed to utilize a variety of physical therapy treatments other than just subluxation procedures. After three weeks of intense therapy procedures, my sciatic nerve pain vanished. I found myself virtually pain free. After five weeks of treatments, I returned to full duties as a police officer. I continued treatments for about a year, gradually lessening the frequency to about one or two a month. My days of missing work were over thanks to the chiropractor and to God's grace. At that time, I didn't see God's hand in things yet, but it was soon to be revealed to me. A whole new journey was about to begin for Al Novak.

After returning to work, I checked with our personnel office to see who this John person was from our workmen's comp program. They told me that they had never heard of a John or sent him out to interview me. Could John have simply been a ministering angel who was sent by God? This remains to be an unsolved mystery. Who was John from workmen's comp?

> "Are not all angels spirits in the divine service, sent to serve for the sake of those who are to inherit salvation?" Hebrews 1:14 (NRSV)

CHAPTER 12

Have You Heard?

My first day back on duty is quite a story. I arrived early for work. Lineup was always ten minutes to the hour, and I was in the squad room half an hour early. It was great to be back with my brothers in blue. We talked about all the things that had been happening while I was on medical leave.

One of the guys asked me if I had heard about Randy.

"Randy?" I questioned. "What about Randy?"

"Yeah, Al, while you were on medical leave, Randy became one of those b-b-b-born-again Christians!"

"What?" I said repeating in a question. "Randy had become a born-again Christian?" I was dumbfounded. I couldn't believe it. Randy was one of the cops on my shift who I didn't like. He had a bad attitude as a police officer, and he treated most people like dirt. I generally rode in a one-man car or would be assigned to train a rookie. I disliked responding to dispatches that Randy had been sent on. Randy would agitate situations with his attitude as he talked down to people, and the situations often turned into fiascos. Many of the cops I worked with

...vidual attitude issues, but Randy had one of the worst in my opinion.

Prior to lineup that day, Randy walked in with a smile on his face carrying what appeared to be a large Bible under his arm. I was totally astonished. The guys chuckled and ridiculed him, but I wasn't joining in yet. I wasn't so sure what it meant to be a born-again Christian, but I remembered my connections with Ron back in the hospital. Ron's faith seemed real enough, but what about Randy? Could his spiritual change also be real?

I was very skeptical about all this religious stuff. After all, I had previously, in the line of duty, arrested priests, nuns, and ministers who acted very religious, but they chose to violate the law. I thought, *Who are these people kidding? Christians!*

I remembered one time receiving a dispatch to check out a suspicious car and occupant. It was about two thirty in the morning, and the house was situated on the corner of the street. A streetlight highlighted the area as I stopped my squad car about half a block away from the scene. I noticed a car parked on the street and a head, silhouetted by the corner streetlight, moving up and down inside the car.

I approached cautiously with my sidearm drawn and my flashlight in hand. Walking up to the car, I shined my flashlight onto the front seat of the car. Up popped a man who was dressed in a suit. I said to him, "What are you doing?"

He started to turn red-faced and said, "Oh, you see, Officer! Well, I am a minister, and I was asked to visit the couple who live in that house. You see, they were having a marriage problem and asked me to come over and talk with them."

"Yeah, so what are you doing out here in the car?"

"Well, you see, I came out to the car to have a cigarette, and they didn't know that I smoked." He lowered his eyes as he confessed his shortcoming.

This added to my preconception that religion was just a big fat hoax. I said, "You *hypocrite*! Who are you kidding? You're a Christian, all right—saying one thing and hiding in a car doing another."

After verifying his identification, I told him to leave the area. I thought about how religious people share that they are living for God, but when you're not looking, they're doing something wrong. *"Christians,"* I thought, *"They don't show me anything!"*

Randy, however, was another story. I was told later that Randy's wife had been praying for him for many years prior for his conversion to Christ. I watched him around the station for several months. Randy was always carrying his Bible and talking about religion to whomever would listen. He was maturing although, as I observed him downgrade from that larger Bible to a smaller medium-sized one. I thought sardonically, *This must be a sign of real spiritual maturity that when you get down to carrying a little pocket testament, you probably have reached the pinnacle of your spiritual growth.*

CHAPTER 13

Have You Asked?

My squad car was in for service on that Monday morning, and Sergeant Nelson assigned me to ride with Randy for the day. I had been observing him around the station on and off for the past four months and listened to the ridicule he received from our fellow officers. I attempted to stay clear and just observe. It would take a lot for me to buy into Randy's religion because of personal skepticism.

When beginning our tour of duty together, we discussed some police issues and carried on with some general conversation. Randy placed his medium-sized Bible on the bench seat between us. We received a radio dispatch to a Woodward Avenue motel on an attempted suicide run. Arriving at the scene, we contacted the motel manager and had him stand by with the door room key if needed. We knocked on the door of the motel room and heard a muffling sound inside but no response to our knocking. The manager provided a key, and we carefully opened the door.

Sitting on the foot of the bed was a man who had to weigh more than four hundred pounds. He was positioned sideways to us with his head bent forward. He looked very despondent. He hadn't shaved or bathed in a month. The room was emanating from extreme body odor stench, and it radiated throughout the entire place.

I expected Randy to handle this individual with his normal disrespectful attitude. I thought he might tell the man that he was garbage and treat him like the same, but Randy didn't do that this time. He walked out to the squad car, grabbed his Bible, and pulled up a chair directly in from of the man. He began to talk to him about his problems. Randy shared with this mam his need of a Savior and offered him hope as he opened his Bible and read some scripture to him.

The man listened intently; he was searching for hope.

I stood by the door, interrupting Randy every five minutes or so. We had a rule on our department that we always had to visually protect our partners. I stood partially on the inside of this putrid-smelling room, staying as close to the door as I could. I leaned my head outside, took a deep breath of fresh air, and told Randy several times to hurry up.

Randy spoke with the man for about twenty minutes. He held the man's hands and prayed with him as I radioed for an ambulance. After the ambulance arrived, we were able to get the man off to the hospital. I wrote up the incident report as we resumed patrol with Randy driving.

I said to him, "Randy, I feel like I am empty inside. I can't put my finger on it, but there is definitely a real void in my life."

He looked at me and said, "I know what you need, Al."

I said, "What?"

"Al, you need Jesus Christ in your life."

I could feel myself begin to swell up on the inside as my defense system shifted into gear. I said, "Look, Randy, I have always believed in Jesus Christ. I was a vocational student and studied for three years and planned on becoming a Roman Catholic priest. Do you think I wouldn't believe in Jesus Christ?" If anyone would have said that to me, I would have fought them in defense of the fact that I believed in Christ. I said, "Randy, I still feel empty deep down inside, and I just can't shake it."

As we continued patrol, Randy said, "Al, let me ask you a question. I really want you to think about this question. Have you ever asked Jesus Christ to be your personal Savior? Have you ever asked Him to forgive you for your sins? Have you ever asked Him to come into your heart and take over your life?"

I said, "You mean, like, actually talk to Him?"

Randy said, "Yeah. Really talk to Him."

"No, Randy, I don't think I have ever done that ... talk to Him personally."

He said, "Well, Al, that's what you need."

I said, "You mean, that's what will get rid of this empty feeling inside?" Randy said, "You will definitely feel different all right."

Randy shared some other Bible verses with me, but I don't know which ones they were. I listened politely, but my mind had become blurred. We talked on and off until the rest of our tour of duty was completed. I thanked Randy for his words, and as I drove home that day, I thought about the things Randy had shared with me. I also thought about how Randy's attitude had changed.

I didn't know it at the time, but Randy told me later that he was very excited about sharing Christ with me. I was the first officer on our shift who sincerely listened to him. He immediately called his pastor when he got home. Randy was attending a small Baptist church in Clawson, and he told his pastor that he had just shared Christ with me and asked him what they should do. His pastor said, "Well, Randy, we will get the whole church praying for Al Novak!"

A dirty trick is when a whole church begins praying for you. For six days, I experienced deep personal conviction and continued to recall all my sins. This conviction within one's soul (mind, intellect, and will) can be a spiritual process of God. Each day, I was more and more aware of being lost and understanding it to be real. Randy's suggestion kept going over and over in my mind: "Al, you need Jesus Christ in your life!" Even while shaving, whistling, and looking in the mirror, I could hear his words clearly in my mind: "You need Jesus Christ in your life!" I just couldn't stop hearing those words. I pounded my head sideways to shake those words out.

After six days under God's conviction power, I was heading to work on southbound I-75. The best way to describe what took place in my car is to examine "genuine communication." Determining throughout one's life there are three levels of communication. The first level of communication is to greet one another. "Hi. How are you doin'?" "Fine." This is a very basic social level of communication, or I would call this the initial greeting level.

The best illustration of second level would be when we share opinions or statements with one another. "Do you think it's going to rain today?" "No. I don't think so." "What was the score of the hockey game last night?" "Red Wings, 5–3." In second level communication, we share our opinions or make statements to one another.

It is much rarer to connect with one another on third level communication. For example, if you were to say to me, "Al, I want to tell you something that is deep within my heart. Will you listen?" I might respond, "I also have something deep within my heart that I want to share with you. Will you listen?" This type of conversation or communication is deeply personal and intimate. Sometimes best of friends like a husband and wife might get there, but we seldom have genuine heart-to-heart conversations with one another at that level. Most of our lives are spent communicating in the first and second levels.

While driving into work that night, I found myself drawn into a deep level of communication with God. I asked Jesus Christ to be *my* Savior (as Randy had told me), and I asked Him to forgive me for all my sins. That was a big request. I asked Him to totally take over *my* life. At that very moment, my life was transmogrified from sinner to saved. I experienced a total removal of this burden of sin that had weighed me down, yes, all my sin was gone. It was my first intimate moment of connecting with God in my life, and I knew that He truly heard my sincere cries of faith in Jesus. By faith I believed in and received Jesus Christ as my own Savior along with the total forgiveness that is granted by God's grace with that decision. We need to remember that God is not just our God but that He is a loving and caring Person too.

The primary purpose of this book is to encourage each one of us to pursue intimacy with God. My spiritual life began when I connected with God intimately. I cried out to Him with all my heart, and He heard me. Later I drifted into various religious traditions, and then adopted legalism as the normal Christian way of life. Learning about grace as I read through the Bible, enabled me to understand that God saves and keeps us by His grace alone. This became my pain reliever from legalism.

Someone once said that if you want people to build ships, give them a love for the ocean. A deepening love for God our Father and His son, Jesus could result in God using us to build ships for His glory. My life, like so many of us, got sidetracked with building ships and lost sight of knowing and loving our heavenly Dad intimately. Often, we substitute our intimate time with God thinking that our performance of Christian works, duties, and responsibilities is what He is after. All God really wants is us! He loves us so much that He simply wants to have alone time with us and hopes that we will make ourselves available to Him.

It normally took me about forty-five minutes to drive from Ortonville to Royal Oak. I must have pulled off I-75 at least three times just weeping before the Lord. I had been made aware of how lost I was and headed for the lake of fire. I was completely disconnected from God and from others. I knew the burden I was under and what God's total forgiveness of sin would mean to me. I wanted God to take over my life because it was in shambles, and He did.

On the outside, my life appeared to be clean and upright, spit and polish, Royal Oak's finest, but deep within my heart, I was no better than the "scum" (as I called them) that I would arrest and put in jail. My nickel-plated Smith & Wesson .357 Magnum that I carried on duty had been polished to a shine. It was mirror clean, and you could see your reflection on the side of the weapon. It was just like my outside appearance; however, on the inside, I knew I was "scummy."

After my intimate encounter with God while driving to work, I arrived at the police station that night and dressed in my full uniform and headed upstairs to the squad room. Next to our line-up room was the employee coffee area. Randy was sitting in there by himself. I walked through the doorway and said, "Randy, I asked Jesus Christ into my life tonight!"

He jumped up excitedly and said, "You did?" He had a big smile as he came up and gave me a bear hug, lifting me off my feet. "Praise the Lord!" He expressed his great joy for me.

Some of our fellow patrolmen were getting ready for lineup in the squad room. They could see us through the doorway, and I could almost sense their cynical questioning, "What is going on between Young and Novak?" Maybe they thought something was going on between us. They had no idea about the new brotherly connection through Christ that we now shared.

Randy handed me a King James Version of the Bible and had it marked with a bookmark at the Gospel of John. He told me that I could have it if I promised to read it.

I said, "I promise, Randy. I will read it."

He told me to read it through slowly from where he had it bookmarked and all the way to the end.

I reassured him that I would. At line-up I was assigned Beat 2. After a thorough check was made of my squad car materials, I left the station and began my tour of duty.

It was a Saturday night, and normally it would be very busy. There were some nights that beat 2 would receive ten to fifteen dispatches. I pulled my squad car into the Shell gas station on the corner of Lincoln Avenue and Main Street and observed the intersection. I opened the Bible that Randy had given me and began to read it.

The very first miracle was that I did not receive my first dispatch until two thirty. I was captivated by what I was reading. Growing up Roman Catholic, I was familiar with portions of the Bible. The Mass and the Sunday homilies would often contain scripture readings that sometimes were difficult to fully understand and apply to my life. But as I read the Bible this time, every word leaped off the page and landed directly in my heart. For the first time I understood what I was reading. It was the strangest thing that I had ever experienced, and it mesmerized my heart.

After completing my tour of duty that night, I went home and continued to read the Bible that Randy had given me. I read it very slowly for months.

One morning, my wife Terri said, "What are you doing?"

I said, "I am reading the Bible."

She said, "What for?"

I said, "I don't know."

She asked why I wasn't going out drinking with the guys on my days off.

I told her that I didn't know and only desired to read the Bible.

Another interesting event occurred during the first week after accepting Jesus as my Savior. I was driving home through a major Michigan winter snowstorm. There were eight or ten inches of heavy snow on the ground and it was still coming down. Road conditions were very poor, and my normal practice was to use profanity and vulgar language, particularly at other drivers. This time, however, was different. I began to focus on the beautiful snow-laden tree branches as I was driving past them and began audibly praising God for how beautiful His snowfall creations were on the trees and rolling hills. *What was going on? What happened to the old Al Novak?*

A remarkable breakthrough also surfaced, in that I no longer desired to drink alcohol. It wasn't the right and wrong of drinking, but peace with God had completely replaced my desire to drink. Never had I thought that this could be possible that one could experience internal peace without booze or drugs.

Drinking often—with the express purpose of getting drunk—was a serious problem for me. Part of my need for alcohol was to forget the terrible things that I had witnessed during my police work. From the viewpoint of a cop, the world is a terrible place to live. So much inhumanity existed in our communities as people would hurt people who were hurting. Alcohol was my logical way of finding some momentary peace inside, but it become apparent that God had a different proposition in store for me.

Some people are mean drunks; however, I was a happy drunk. Everybody liked me drunk, and I was kind of like the life of the party. I had made many bar friends over the years, and I had a personal charge card issued to me through the Roman Gate Lounge in Royal Oak where I regularly patronized. My salvation experience contained an unexpected set of events, and one of those was the total elimination of any need for a strong drink. It was difficult to make sense of what had happened to me. My drinking habits cost me well over five thousand dollars per year in bar tabs. I used to work two or three part-time (off-duty) jobs to pay my bar tabs. This had become a serious issue and now I no longer needed nor wanted to drink. For a while I missed the fellowship from many of my bar friends after abandoning my bar seat. But God had placed in my heart a genuine peace that I was not willing to surrender for anyone or any reason. Thank you, Lord for this amazing rest within my soul!

CHAPTER 14

Candy Van

Don (not his real name) was a former bar acquaintance who became a friend. Don happened to be the general manager of a local radio station. This event took place in my pre-Christ days. One evening, we were drinking together and talking about stuff. Often, I found the loneliest people were those who hung out at the bar. They became my best buddies since I also needed someone to dialogue with who had the time.

Don was telling me about his radio station's latest promotion. Not being a listener to his station at all, I really knew nothing about his promo. He began to tell me that his station was having a contest with a brand-new Dodge cargo van that was partially full of assorted candy bars in the rear cargo space. Most of the candy bars were comprised of an assortment of smaller-sized Milky Way, Snickers, Three Musketeers, M&M's, and Twix. Anyone who could guess the total weight of the van with the candy bars inside could win the van and all the candy in it.

As we conversed about the radio station promo, Don asked me about my pay as a police officer. He mentioned in the form of a question if I could use a van due to the needs of having a family with three kids. I kind of nodded in a positive way but was not really interested in guessing the weight.

He said to me, "I am the only one who knows the weight of the van since I had it weighed myself." He suggested that he could share with me the correct weight and have me mail in a postcard with that weight—and then I would win the van. Feeling a bit odd about it, he did convince me that I really could use this vehicle and I agreed. He thought that I of all people deserved it as a fine, upstanding police officer. He said, "Somebody is going to win this van—and why shouldn't it be you?"

He told me the weight of the van and had me write it down: 4,853 pounds. He told me to send in ten postcards to the radio station with one of them containing the correct weight. So, without really thinking it through, I followed his suggestions.

After a few months, I received a call from the radio station that informed me I was a finalist in the contest. There was scheduled to be a final public drawing at the shopping mall for all the finalists with the promotional fanfare that was included by the radio station.

A bit puzzled by this information, Don called and told me that ten people had guessed the correct weight. He told me to send him ten additional postcards with the correct weight on each card ASAP. I did what he requested, but I really did not know what was going on.

On the day of the drawing I went to the mall and was invited up on the stage with the other finalists. Don was standing behind me, and he whispered in my ear that I was going to win the van. I did not know what had transpired, but I found out later that Don had put all ten of my winning numbered postcards in the box—alone. So, he knew that I was going to win for sure. My odds were a 100 percent to win.

Someone from the station reached in the box, pulled out a card, and announced that the winner was Al Novak. I was interviewed live on the radio station and acted completely surprised about winning the candy van. They also acknowledged that I was a police officer with a wife and three kids. It was all done so smoothly, and they handed me the keys to the van with all the candy inside.

I drove the van home to our newly self-built house in Ortonville. My uncle was a builder and a cement contractor, and he guided and taught me house construction skills.

When I arrived home, I started looking through the back of the van. I found large cardboard candy boxes underneath all the candy bars. After I pulled out all the empty boxes, there was still a considerable amount of candy there, but it was not as much as it appeared.

Our son Michael was around seven years old at the time. He looked at all the candy bars in the back of the van. He was usually the first one to jump into any adventure. He crawled on top of all the candy bars and swam around like Scrooge McDuck swimming in his millions. He just wallowed in the back of the van amid all the candy bars in a euphoric stage of excitement of total happiness. We packed all the candy bars into the original boxes and stacked them in the garage.

After a short while, my conscience began to bother me. Being raised with good moral standards, I decided that we should give away all the candy bars to an orphanage. We loaded up all the candy bars, with our kids sad and crying, and drove the van to a distant Catholic orphanage.

I thought by giving the candy away it would ease my conscience. I did consider myself to be an upright person and an honorable police officer, and this did help for a short time.

My conscience bothered me, but not necessarily from receiving the candy van. It was the time spent away from my family during my adamant drinking days that became my real issue. I felt guilty about being so selfish and committed to staying on my road of perdition.

Shortly after I received Jesus Christ as my personal Savior, things began to really change in my heart. Within the first week, God began to deal with me about accepting that candy van. I sensed a relentless spiritual pressure in my heart that God was directing me to confess my part in the process of acquiring the van.

Randy now was my spiritual advisor and father in the faith, and I told him about the pressure I was sensing from God to confess my part in the contest scam. Randy told me that all my sins were now under the blood of Christ, and they had been forgiven the very moment I put all my faith and trust in Christ. The blood of Christ had washed away all my sin, according to the Bible. Randy gave me correct spiritual advice, but God would not let up on me for some reason. I prayed for days, but there was no relief. God's pressure to confess was heavy upon my heart and spirit.

After several weeks of praying about the matter, I decided that I must confess my part. The van contest had taken place several years prior to my salvation experience, and I had sold the van and purchased another family vehicle to replace it. Don had taken another manager's position at a radio station that was a long distance away, and we had lost contact with one another over the years.

I called the radio station that had originally promoted the candy van contest and asked to speak with the manager. I told him that I wanted to talk with him and confess something. He asked me if he needed lawyers present during our meeting, and I told him that it was his call. We set a meeting time and date.

I arrived at the radio station at the appointed time and met with the manager. I explained the whole thing to him about winning the van and being informed of the correct weight. It had been years since the event occurred, and he did not remember the promotion giveaway at all. After I brought him up to date, he was puzzled about why I would confess to him after all this time had passed. I told him about my salvation experience and explained that God wanted me to confess it.

My offer to him and the radio station was full restitution for the cost of the van and all the candy bars. I was willing to take out a loan so the radio station could offer another van contest.

He said he would contact his lawyers and seek their advice. I told him that I would most likely be fired if he called my police chief. However, it was up to him. I would not object to whatever path he chose to follow to reconcile the matter. He had a very puzzled look upon his face as I left his office that day. He said that he would get back with me and that this information was to remain between us at this time.

Immediately after getting back to my car, the enormous pressure that God had placed on my heart to confess was completely gone. I felt total relief. All I could do was praise the Lord! Regardless of the outcome, I knew that I had done what He had asked me to do. His peace returned and flooded my soul. A new realization took over as I became completely assured that I could trust the Lord even though the results were not completely known yet.

After a few weeks, the radio station manager called and asked me to meet with him again in his office. When the meeting began, he said that he had spoken with his legal staff, and they had decided to completely drop the matter. He did not want any restitution for the van, but I offered it to him again. He was still puzzled about why I had confessed. I again informed him that God alone was the reason for my confession.

We shook hands as I started to leave, and he said that he had one more question: "Who gave you the correct weight of the van?" As I shared with him that my purpose was to confess my part in the scheme, and I would not reveal the name of the other person. He continued with further questions about the person who gave me the van weight, and again I refused to answer. My same response to his question was that I came to reveal my part of the scheme only. He finally gave up and I left that day, thanking God for his favor in resolution of this matter.

There is an addendum to this story. Shortly after I received Jesus as my Savior, I sent out a nine-page letter to each of my friends and family members, sharing my salvation experience along with a gospel invitation. My hope was for all my friends and family members to find peace with God.

After sending out the letters, I prayed to God that these would fall upon fertile soil. I prayed that just one recipient might be saved from reading my letter but only asked for one. Don was one of my friends who received my letter. I heard nothing back in response from anyone, but I continued to pray for all those who had received it.

Several months later, Don called me up. He said that he had received my letter and read it over and over again for a month. He was asked by another friend to attend a full-Gospel businessman's meeting. At that meeting, an invitation was given—and Don accepted Christ as his Savior. He said his whole life had changed, and my letter had guided him to make that decision. He was eternally grateful and sounded so full of joy. I rejoiced with him at the good news of his salvation.

The story doesn't end there. Months later, the manager that I confessed to was attending a meeting of the metropolitan Detroit area radio station managers. Don was at that meeting also and knew this man. Don went up to him at the meeting—not knowing of our previous connections—and confessed that he had unjustly given the weight of the radio station's Dodge candy van to a friend of his. Don told him that God had asked him to confess this information to him.

The station manager was under such conviction after both of our unsolicited confessions that he told Don that he wanted to know this God and meet Jesus Christ.

Don rejoiced in leading him to Christ that very day. That is why my answer to God is always yes! He only asks us to be available to Him. He does all the work. After all, it is God's will that all men be saved:

> "For this is good and acceptable in the sight of God our Savior, who desires all men to be saved and to come to the knowledge of the truth." 1 Timothy 2: 3–4 (NKJV)

CHAPTER 15

Explaining It to Terri

Everything became new (2 Corinthians 5:17) in my life after I received Jesus Christ as my Savior, but I could not explain it theologically to anyone. I thought I might have Randy and his wife, Donna, come out to visit and explain my salvation experience to Terri. I wanted Terri to know what had happened, but I really didn't understand it myself at the time.

We scheduled a visit and invited them out for the evening. After dinner was completed—along with some casual conversation—the table was cleared. Randy and Donna began to share from God's Word with us. They were zealous about winning Terri to Christ—maybe a bit too zealous! They pummeled her with scripture verses and concluded with a compelling invitation for her to be saved.

The actual word "saved" can be a very negative word for Roman Catholics. We were always taught to believe that no one could know for sure that they were "saved" and that believing this is committing the sin of presumption. Terri had seriously considered in her youth the possibility of becoming a Catholic nun. She was a very devout Catholic and faithfully attended St. Anne's in Ortonville. The scriptures that Randy and Donna shared were very revealing and clearly suggested of her need to receive Jesus Christ as her personal Savior.

Even though Randy and Donna meant well and were concerned about Terri's spiritual well-being, they came on too assertive concerning her need to be "saved." Terri was turned off, especially when they spoke about Mary not being our mediator in prayer. It offended Terri that anyone would slant Mary since she is perceived by Catholics as the mother of God. We both had held Mary in highest esteem, believed her to be our Co-Redemptrix, and prayed to her often and through the rosary. Randy shared this verse from the Bible:

> "For there is one God, and one mediator between God and men, the man Christ Jesus." 1 Timothy 2:5 (NKJV)

That was a verse I had never heard before. I know Terri was greatly impacted by it as well. We were both learning so much about what the Bible really teaches.

By the time they left, Terri was very agitated. She was gracious to them, but I could tell that she was upset. After they were gone, she told me that she did not want to have them over again. She felt intimidated and humiliated as a Catholic. She felt that she was not a bad person and that the Catholic Church could not be that wrong.

I began to pray and ask God for wisdom about how to relate to her that salvation was not found in a "religion" but in a "relationship" with God through Jesus Christ, and that's what made the difference in my life. Much prayer for Terri was needed to enable her to search out for herself this resolution process with God, and I set forth to pray continuously.

Several months went by, and I continued to read the Bible and pray during all my free time. I had not been attending the Catholic church very much due to a confrontation with a priest many years prior concerning the tactics of the Detroit police during the Detroit riots in 1967. After the riots were over, a liberal priest from Detroit was sent to our parish in Royal Oak to establish neighborhood councils with a goal of seeking peace. The statistical facts and information that he presented during his homily at each Mass concerning the actions of the Detroit Police Department and the National Guard were verifiably false. Also, the information I had received from the FBI during my in-service police training classes proved that these allegations and anti-police rhetoric that he shared in his sermons were mostly untrue, which angered me as a police officer. I had stopped attending our Catholic church that day, but Terri remained a faithful follower during all those years.

I continued to read the Bible and found scriptures that contradicted many of the teachings of Catholicism. I began to compare the scriptures with many of my former beliefs. The more I studied, the more convinced I became about my need to depart from formal religion and pursue a deeper relationship with God through the study of God's Word.

I continued to share my scriptural discoveries with Terri, and she graciously listened. She questioned me on many points, and I often had to submit those questions to Randy for the answers. He often would tell me that he would get back with me the next day with the answer. Randy didn't know all the answers either since he was a newer believer, and he kept calling his pastor day and night, with the questions that Terri and I had concerning the Bible. Finally, frustrated over the many late-night calls, Randy's pastor suggested that he needed more biblical training and should register in the Moody Bible Institute's correspondence Bible study course. So, Randy did.

The questions continued for more than two years, and Randy continued to faithfully disciple me. We would meet up on patrol just to pray together and share God's Word whenever we could during quieter times. Randy not only led me to Jesus, but he remained faithful to our Lord's commission: "Go therefore and make disciples" (Matthew 28:19 NASB).

One day I asked Randy a very puzzling theological question, he immediately showed me the exact scripture without hesitation, and it answered my question completely. I later learned that scripture does teach scripture.

I was amazed. I said, "Randy, you are the most knowledgeable person in the scriptures I have ever known. How did you get so much Bible knowledge?"

He looked at me and said, "Al, I'm not as smart as you think!" He told me about going to his pastor day in and day out with my Bible questions and how his pastor had finally told him to take the Moody Bible Institute course. So, he did. It cost him $350 to purchase the course. He was studying two or three hours a night, burning the midnight oil, and getting ready for my next question. He said, "Truly, Al, I am only about two weeks ahead of you in my studies."

The amazing fact was that Randy had spiritually grown tremendously through discipling me, a new believer, requiring him to search the scriptures daily to answer all my theological questions. I was very eager to know the truth. God's instruction to all of us is found in God's Word:

> "But grow in the grace and knowledge of our Lord and Savior Jesus Christ." 2 Peter 3:18 (NKJV)

This does require some diligent study and a Christian should be a faithful student of the Word so that they can handle it correctly:

> "Be diligent to present yourself approved to God, a worker who does not need to be ashamed, rightly dividing the word of truth." 2 Timothy 2:15 (NKJV)

> "Do your best to present yourself to God as one approved, a worker who does not need to be ashamed and who correctly handles the word of truth." 2 Timothy 2:15 (NIV)

Two months after I received Christ as my Savior and experienced a new spiritual birth, Terri recognized that she had always been trying to worm her way into God's favor by doing good works. If anyone, by their good works, could find their way into God's favor, Terri surely would have gained her spot, but she discovered that God's Word was very clear:

> "For by grace you have been saved through faith, and this is not your own doing; it is the gift of God—**not the result of works**, so that no one may boast." (Ephesians 2:8–9 NRSV)

We knelt by the side of our bed one evening, and Terri—by grace through faith—asked Jesus Christ to be her personal Savior. We embraced and wept together with joy that night. It was the first night that we were fully united in our marriage as one. We were not just legally united; we were united in body, soul, and spirit as well. Christ had become the Lord of our personal lives, and now He was the head of our marriage. It was the first time in eighteen years that we truly clicked together as husband and wife. Jesus does make all the difference!

CHAPTER 16

Christian Cops Meet

Several weeks after I accepted the Lord, Randy invited me to attend a meeting of the Michigan Fellowship of Christian Police Officers.

I said, "Are you serious? Christian cops? You mean, actually, the born-again kind?"

He said, "Yes."

I thought, *Imagine the possibility of other cops—besides Randy and me—being born again!*

Randy told me how the group met once a month at different locations. On Tuesday, they were meeting at Tabernacle Baptist Church in Hazel Park. He said, "Will you come?"

I told him that I would think about it, and it did sound very interesting.

When the day arrived, I decided to go. I pulled into the parking lot behind the church and just sat in my car. I was kind of hoping Randy would arrive and take me by the hand. I started to get out of my car twice, but I sat back down both times. I had never been in a Baptist church, and I thought, *I wonder if they sacrifice dogs or cats in there.* I honestly didn't know what a Baptist church did for worship.

Being quite certain that God prompted me to exit my car after this ten-minute battle of the mind, I entered the building. A posted sign directed me to the meeting room.

At the entrance, a short man with a big smile was greeting the arrivals. He shook my hand and said, "Hi, I'm Brad with the Troy Police Department." That was a neighboring city to the northeast of Royal Oak.

I introduced myself and told him that Randy Young had invited me to come to the meeting.

He took me inside the room and introduced me to thirty-five full-time law enforcement officers who were sitting in an oval and talking to one another. The meeting was about to begin, and Randy had still not arrived.

Present in the room were an FBI agent, an Alcohol-Tax-Tobacco Division agent, several sheriff deputies from different counties in Michigan, city police officers from a variety of departments around Michigan, Michigan State Police Troopers—some being command officers—and there was even a chief of police from a metro-Detroit city. I was greeted by all.

They started at my right, and the officers shared how they had come to know Jesus Christ as their Savior and how their lives had been changed from darkness to light. *Cops!* I was amazed beyond measure.

As one Michigan State Officer, assigned to an undercover narcotics unit, began to share, I noticed tears rolling into his beard. He was a burly fellow with tattoos on his arms and a .45 automatic stuck inside his hip. I couldn't believe it. Cops who were really saved and born again—and anxious to share what Jesus Christ meant to them.

As the meeting concluded, they all stood to pray. Gripping one another's hands, some began to alternately pray audibly. As they prayed, I prayed to myself. I really do not know what they were praying, but I said, "Dear Father in heaven, you have made Jesus become totally real to me today through my fellow officers, and I am at a loss as to what to do. Lord, I feel compelled to do something for You! The only thing I know to do is to offer myself to You. So, dear heavenly Father, I offer myself to you unconditionally with no strings attached. Please do with me whatever you wish. I will go wherever you want me to go and do whatever you want me to do."

As they said, "Amen," I did also.

I thought, *Oh, no! Novak, don't you know what you just did? You are going to have to go to Sears and buy a canoe, a paddle, a flyswatter, and some Gospel tracts because you are going up the Amazon River, buddy! Anyone who makes a commitment to God like that will surely end up in a foreign mission somewhere—most likely in a remote jungle.*

Obviously, I was wrong as God recognized my offer as an acceptable sacrifice for service:

> "I beseech you therefore, brethren, by the mercies of God, that you present your bodies a living sacrifice, holy, acceptable to God, which is your reasonable service." (Romans 12:1 NKJV)

God's acceptance of my sacrifice to Him did not involve the jungles of Africa, but He did begin to change my whole thinking process about criminals—and ultimately down the road a desire to take His love to those incarcerated behind bars.

Wow, talk about the empowerment of God! When I left that MFCPO meeting, I knew something was different. The power of God was all over me. There was an infilling that was truly supernatural, and boldness seemed to permeate my entire being. There was no longer any fear about witnessing for Jesus as my spirit was exploding with excitement. I was bubbling over with enthusiasm to share my faith with someone—anyone! I wanted others to know the joy and peace that I had received from God. I could hardly contain myself, like a rock was about to break open and speak.

> "Yes, all the things I once thought were so important are gone from my life. Compared to the high privilege of knowing Christ Jesus as my Master, firsthand, everything I once thought I had going for me is insignificant—dog dung. I've dumped it all in the trash so that I could embrace Christ and be embraced by him. I didn't want some petty, inferior brand of righteousness that comes from keeping a list of rules when I could get the robust kind that comes from trusting Christ—God's righteousness."
> Philippians 3:8–9 (The Message)

CHAPTER 17

Testing Begins

I left the MFCPO meeting and headed directly to the police station arriving early for work. As I waited until 10:50 p.m. for line-up to begin, I sat near my locker and thought about the events of the evening with the Christian cops. It was like tasting something spiritually invigorating to have joined the ranks of Christian cops. My mind kept rolling over the testimonies of those officers at the meeting and how God was using them to be "lights" in a dark world.

Dressing slowly into my uniform, all I could think about was the meeting that I had just attended. The very last thing in preparation for my tour of duty was to examine and dry-fire my .357 Magnum. It was a department-issued nickel-plated Smith & Wesson Model 19, and I kept it very clean and polished. It reminded me of the new life that I was now experiencing in Christ. I checked the cylinder of the weapon and made sure the cartridges were spendable. I checked all the moveable parts of the revolver to make sure everything was in working order and then re-holstered.

My thoughts also reminded me that God was now in control of my life since I gave it to Him, and I could now enjoy His Fatherly protection as His child. Peace flooded my soul, and the security of this new intimate relationship with God began to grow. I was so hungry to know more about God and to comprehend our new love relationship that He had been patiently waiting to initiate. I also recognized that every time I put on my police uniform, it was for an honorable purpose. The Constitution of the United States of America authorized me (if necessary) to instantaneously take a human life in the performance of my duties of protecting and serving the citizens of our community. This is absolute power over life and death! I knew that when a police officer had to make that instant decision to kill someone in the performance of his duties that the courts would then spend six months deciding whether it was justified or not. God's power was certainly greater than mine, and my fear was no longer in man. I thought of a verse that I had read that day:

> "And do not fear those who kill the body but cannot kill the soul. But rather fear Him who is able to destroy both soul and body in hell." Matthew 10:28 (NKJV)

At lineup, I was assigned Stan as my senior partner for the night. He was a good officer, and I liked Stan and enjoyed riding with him. As we began our tour of duty, I started to tell him about what had transpired spiritually in my life during the past few weeks. I shared with him how I asked Jesus Christ to be my personal Savior and then continued to explain the details of the meeting with the Christian cops.

My whole person radiated with so much joy that my sharing coursed into preaching! Yes, I started to preach to Stan unplanned as God's empowerment seemed to be overflowing and bursting out of me. It was certainly not my intention to burn his ears for the entire eight hours of duty time. We would stop for a lunch break, and I would carry in my Bible (the one Randy gave me). I sat next to him while we ate lunch and preached to him from the Bible. As he was eating, I noticed perspiration forming on his forehead. I honestly believe it wasn't me; the spirit of Christ was speaking to him through me as His vessel. My only desire for Stan was that he would find this peace with God that I was experiencing. This anointing from God was very powerful.

As we neared the station that morning to finish our tour of duty, Stan stopped the squad car about a block away. He looked at me and said, "Al, do you believe all this stuff that you have been telling me all night?"

I began to preach again, but he abruptly interrupted me.

"Just yes or no, Al!"

I said, "Yes, Stan, with all my heart, I believe it."

He said, "OK, Al. Don't say anymore."

We drove into the station, and Stan rushed in ahead of me. He walked up to the front desk where Sgt. Nelson was sitting. He said, "Sarge, whatever you do, never assign me to ride with Novak again. He has snapped and become some religious fanatic. I never want to ride with him again."

> "My brothers and sisters, whenever you face trials of any kind, consider it nothing but joy, because you know that the testing of your faith produces endurance; and let endurance have its full effect, so that you may be mature and complete, lacking in nothing." James 1:2–5 (NRSV)

My time of testing began, and it was no longer easy fitting in with my fellow officers. Each officer I would ride with conveyed the very same rejection as Stan. Even though my longing for them was that they might know the peace within that I was enjoying; however, I regrettably and inadvertently beat them over the head with the Bible. My concerns for their spiritual welfare were blameless, but my methodology was very wrong. As I continued to grow in my Christian faith, the realization started to set in that God was in the saving business—not Al Novak. I had so much to learn in those beginning days of my new faith walk, and persecution became my basic training in wisdom (a. k. a. God's perspective on everything).

My fellow officers dismissed my witness to them, so I would share with waitresses, street people, contacts along the way, and all my family and friends. My compelling desire was for everyone to know God's love, which had totally changed my life. This spiritual re-birth enabled me to find genuine intimacy with God that I had been longing for all my life.

God's grace continued to bring me under His control, but it also required the study of His Word. Sometimes new believers become overly zealous as they attempt to share their faith. I certainly made many mistakes in those early days with my friends. Even my parents and brothers stood against me as they planted their feet more deeply into Roman Catholicism. I did ask God to forgive me for being self-impassioned with my evangelism approaches. As the scriptures became my teacher, I understood that God wanted me to simply be available to Him as opportunities arrived to share my faith. I no longer beat a dead horse but just waited upon Him to open the right doors. Our wonderful heavenly Father graciously granted me another opportunity with each of my fellow officers over the next several years to share Christ with them.

I decided to live my life as a Christian before my fellow officers and friends and wait for them to inquire. Several did and became believers as God drew them to Himself and opened their hearts.

These are things that most of us learn as we move forward after being born into a new spiritual realm of genuine faith and trust in the Lord and we learn that only Jesus saves.

There were so many things to learn ahead as Jesus forewarned:

> "Truly I tell you, there is no one who has left house or brothers or sisters or mother or father or children or fields, for my sake and for the sake of the good news, who will not receive a hundredfold now in this age—houses, brothers and sisters, mothers and children, and fields, with persecutions—and in the age to come eternal life. But many who are first will be last, and the last will be first." Mark 10:29–30 (NRSV)

CHAPTER 18

Smoking Obstacle

During my growing up years, we always looked up to those who smoked cigarettes. Smoking was cool back then, and everyone who smoked was cool. My dad smoked, but he was a very conscientious smoker. He might have smoked maybe three cigarettes a day, but that was about it. I do not think he was addicted to nicotine as most smokers find themselves.

As a fourteen-year-old, I would often borrow a few cigarettes from my dad's pack of Marlboros, also known as stealing. Jerome and I would go out in the woods and smoke them, acting cool as we would swing our arms around, holding a lit cigarette in our hands and puffing on them of course without inhaling. Oh yeah, very cool!

By the time I was seventeen years old, I learned to inhale the smoke and became addicted to the nicotine. As a high school student living in an all-boy's boarding school, I would smoke late at night in our dorm room by blowing the smoke out the window and got away with it. After transferring to St. Mary's of Royal Oak, the juniors, and seniors were permitted to gather across the street, and stand on the street corner, and smoke. We were the cool crowd, and the high school smoking group became my people.

I continued smoking years into my police career. They began to publish new information that cigarette smoking might be dangerous to your health. My attempt to quit many times during those years always ended up in failure. My addiction to nicotine was extremely powerful and nearly impossible to just quit cold turkey.

I recall one day on patrol, I decided to quit smoking. I tucked my pack of cigarettes in the visor over my head in the squad car and made a firm decision to quit and throw them away as soon as I could find a trash bin. Just then I received a dispatch that there was an armed robbery in progress, and shots had been fired. I was about two miles away from the scene, and I responded to the call. I immediately headed in the direction of the reported robbery in progress.

En route to the scene, I unconsciously reached up over the visor, pulled out a cigarette, and lit it up. I thought, *Well, this could be my last cigarette if things don't go well—and I get all shot up.* I tried to quit many times but withdrawal seemed very unlikely. There was always a reason why I would continue to smoke.

One day while getting dressed in the locker room, a fellow officer—and former marine—said, "Novak, give me one of your cigarettes!" I handed him one from my pack. Ted took my cigarette, stood it on end with the filter at the bottom, and placed it on the bench. He barked out a marine style order for me to stand next to that cigarette.

I did as he told me and played along.

He said, "Now stand at attention!"

I put my shoulders back and stood up straight as he commanded.

He said, "Now look down at that cigarette."

I glanced down while standing at attention.

He said, "That tiny little cigarette is stronger than you are and has completely beaten you into submission!"

Smiling and nodding my head in sad agreement with Ted's summation, I realized that that little cigarette was stronger than my determination and willpower to quit. Yes, that cigarette had beaten me into submission time and time again. I had been completely unsuccessful with every attempt to quit.

Even after my new spiritual re-birth experience, I continued to smoke cigarettes as normal, not really thinking about my addiction. Six months had passed by, and my smoking habit remained intact. As a former Catholic, smoking and drinking were quite acceptable; however, this was not true in most conservative Christian camps as I was soon to learn.

My patrol assignment that day was to partner up with Rick, a senior officer. As always, my desire was to look for opportunities to share Christ, especially with my fellow officers. We talked throughout most of the night about religious topics, and I shared my new personal faith in Jesus. Rick was a nominal Roman Catholic, and I completely empathized where he stood on his religious beliefs.

As we were ready to complete our night shift tour of duty together, I said, "Rick, what is preventing you from asking Jesus Christ to be your personal Savior?"

He didn't answer me immediately.

I reached into my top pocket, pulled out a cigarette without a thought, and lit one up.

He looked at me and said, "Al, you are not even a Christian! Don't you know that Christians don't smoke!" He was referring to the born-again kind of Christian who he had only heard about.

I said, "Do you mean that you will not accept Christ as your Savior because I am smoking a cigarette?"

He said, "Yeah, you aren't a Christian because Christians don't smoke!"

When he said that, I realized that my smoking impasse had become a real obstacle in my new walk of faith.

The next day, I was assigned a north end beat as a one-man unit. Being new to this God thing relationship, I would often just talk out loud with God audibly. As I drove around on duty that evening, my heart was deeply troubled. I kept thinking about Rick's response to the Gospel invitation. I told God how sorry I was that Rick would not accept His Son because of my cigarette smoking. I did not see it as a scriptural issue—or whether it was right or wrong to smoke—but Rick rejected Jesus Christ because he perceived me not to be a genuine Christian because of my actions.

As I talked out loud to God in my patrol car, I reminded Him that I really had tried to quit smoking on my own but was unable to stop. I said to my Father, "If you show me how to quit, I will do so; nevertheless, may I say that all of my past efforts have failed, as You know—adding that my prayer to Him was in Jesus' name."

I drove over to Northwood Shopping Center and decided to purchase a pack of chewing gum. Parking my squad car in front of Cunningham's Drug Store, I walked directly in and up to the cashier counter. Selecting a pack of gum and waiting to pay, I noticed a sign up over the head of the cashier. The poster displayed "One Step at a Time" filters with a price tag of $9.99 and a large slash over the listed price. The handwritten visible closeout price was $7.00.

Asking the cashier about the filters, she informed me that they were designed to help a person quit smoking. I asked her how many packets she had in stock, and she informed me that there was only one left. Looking in my wallet to see how much money was there, yes, you guessed it, I had exactly seven dollars in my wallet.

I put two and two together very quickly—since I had just asked God five minutes earlier to show me how to quit smoking—that maybe this was His answer. Informing the cashier that I needed to purchase her last "One Step" packet, she handed it to me with a puzzled look on her face. Giving her all the cash money left in my wallet, I proceeded to leave the store.

The One-Step (eight-week) program contained instructions and included four pre-filters. The directions were to continue smoking the same number of cigarettes but place each cigarette into the pre-filter before lighting up. The first two-week phase filter reduced the nicotine and tars in the cigarette by about 25 percent and the second filter reduced the nicotine and tars by 50 percent. The phase 3 filter was a 75 percent reduction, and then phase 4, the final filter, would remove 90 percent.

Each filter required periodic flushing with water as to the percentage of nicotine and tar removal. The first filter was about every two days. Then the second filter required each day. Phase 3 was about every tenth cigarette and phase 4 was about every second or third cigarette. My brand of cigarettes were Camel filters, and they were a bit stronger than Winston or Marlboro.

Remaining faithful to the program and graduating every two weeks to the next phase, I continued to smoke my normal one to two packs per day. Cigarettes were very affordable and only cost about twenty-five cents a pack back then.

After my seventh week, and halfway through phase 4, I began to flush out the filter and all the nicotine and tars from only three cigarettes that I had smoked through that filter. The area was brightly illuminated with fluorescent lighting, and the wash basins were bright white. This filter phase removed 90 percent of the nicotine and tars, which were dripping out of the filter. At the bottom of the sink, I began to observe the swirling water mixed with this black and dark brown, gooey, and smelly residue.

At that exact moment, God spoke clearly to my heart. I suddenly became aware with a fresh awareness for the first time that this terrible-smelling residue of the nicotine and tars were entering my body and causing danger to my physical health. He also made me very mindful of the scripture that spoke of my body now becoming His property and it was purchased at a high cost. I needed to care for it responsibly:

> You say, "I am allowed to do anything"—but not everything is good for you. And even though "I am allowed to do anything," I must not become a slave to anything." 1 Corinthians 6:12 (NLT)

> "Don't you realize that your body is the temple of the Holy Spirit, who lives in you and was given to you by God? You do not belong to yourself, for God bought you with a high price. So, you must honor God with your body." 1 Corinthians 6:19–20 (NLT)

It was clear that God wanted me to see His point about taking care of His property since I offered myself to Him with no strings attached. My understanding of His scriptural truths became very clear. It was at that moment, without any hesitation, I tossed the rest of the pack of cigarettes and my lighter into the trash—and I never smoked another cigarette again.

Even after a year, if someone smoked a cigarette around me, there was still a brief temptation. Now after all these years of being free from the bondage of nicotine that just the smell of a cigarette anywhere near me is extremely unpleasant and very repulsive to me.

I am grateful that restaurants started to offer non-smoking sections and ultimately banned smoking completely in public restaurants and in most public places. Even secondhand smoke is dangerous to your health. Food tastes very bad to me when cigarette smoke is anywhere nearby.

Thank You, Lord, for freeing me from this terrible bondage that was so prevalent in the destruction of my body. May the results bring You glory! Amen.

The lesson learned in my early Christian days was that when you ask for God's help and follow His directions, do not forget that all honor and glory for the victory should be given to Him alone.

On my own, I could not quit smoking, but when I submitted to His guidance, God made the seemingly impossible very possible and attainable. He did it by opening my eyes and gently revealing to me what cigarette smoke was doing to my body. The poisonous nicotine and tars had been entering my body with each cigarette and destroying it. Our heavenly Father knows best!

A great price had been paid for mine and your spiritual freedom from the bondage of sin. The payment was made in full when Jesus died on the cross for us and shed all His blood. He is our Savior and our Lord whether we accept Him or not. Receiving His offer of complete forgiveness for our sins enables us to become part of the family of God and find peace amidst our troubles. It all boils down to simply trusting in Jesus and accepting his offer. Followship (a. k. a. following Jesus as our Lord) became a new spiritual direction that offers us another peace that we cannot fully understand that will be discussed in the next chapter.

When we truly hand our problems over to God and wait upon Him to show us the way; the solution will be fulfilling, final, and complete. God is Love, and He is always on our side. May I say that God is not the one who comes to kill, steal, and destroy. He sent One namely, Jesus, to bring us an abundant life here and now and in the days to come:

> "The thief comes only to steal and kill and destroy. I came that they may have life, and have it abundantly."
> John 10:10 (NRSV)

CHAPTER 19

The Peace of God

As a new believer, I was committed to reading the Bible daily. It took me around two and a half months reading from the Gospel of John, word for word, before I arrived at the book of Philippians. Having no desire for any alcoholic beverages all that time was surprising to me. Somehow, this spiritual puzzle that I was living in had afforded me a release from my serious drinking problem. For example, one watering hole (AKA Roman Gate Lounge) that I drank in tabbed me at more than five thousand dollars in one year. Working several part-time jobs enabled me to pay my bar tabs along with providing our family needs. This was a very serious problem in my life.

The common plight for seemingly all humans is finding peace in our lives, the kind of peace that enables our hearts to rest from our daily struggles. Most of our lives this appears to slip through our fingers. Yes, I did find moments of superficial peace through excessive drinking. However now, for the first time in my life, I was enjoying continual peace without the booze. So, what was the reason for this?

When I read Philippians 4:6–7 (see last paragraph in this

chapter), I discovered the answer to my question as to why I no longer desired any strong drink. My excessive and repetitive drinking represented a search for genuine peace—just as it did for most of my drinking buddies. We were all looking for the exact same thing. I discovered that there is no lasting peace in this world apart from having Jesus:

> "I have told you these things, so that in me you may have peace. In this world you will have trouble. But take heart! I have overcome the world." John 16:33 (NIV)

The Bible speaks of two kinds of peace: the peace *with* God and the peace *of* God. Have you made your peace with God? In other words, have you asked Jesus Christ to be your personal Savior and know for certain that all your sins are forgiven? Those who put their faith and trust in Jesus Christ have been declared not guilty by God are now at peace *with* Him:

> "Therefore being justified by faith, we have peace with God through our Lord Jesus Christ." Romans 5:1 (KJV)

For a clearer explanation on finding peace with God and receiving Christ, please go to billygraham.com/watch some of the Billy Graham TV classics and videos on YouTube or listen to the Billy Graham channel on SiriusXM. I might suggest that you consider purchasing some of his books online or at Christian bookstores. These suggested aids and locations will help you on your way of finding peace with God. This is the first step to finding intimacy with God and all must begin here by receiving Jesus as your personal Savior. Remember that touching first base is a must for the win.

In 1924, "Goose" Goslin established himself as one of the top run producers in Major League Baseball. He also helped his team, the Washington Senators, get to the World Series in back-to-back seasons and win their first world championship.

During one of those World Series games, a major blunder took place. The score was tied late in the game, and Goslin was at the plate with two outs. He hit a deep fly ball that hit the top of the outfield wall and bounced back into the field of play. The ball danced around the outfield a bit as Goslin rounded the bases in pursuit of an inside-the-park home run. The fans launched out of their seats. All eyes were fastened on home plate as the shortstop took the cutoff from left center, rotated, and fired the ball to the catcher. Goslin slid into home, whipping up a cloud of dust—well before the tag—and the plate umpire called him safe.

The crowd became delirious, but the hysteria of the fans was shockingly interrupted when the first base umpire came charging in and declared that Goslin had missed first base. Thereby, he was ruled out.

After the game, a reporter grabbed Goslin and said, "Goose, didn't you know you had missed first base?"

Goslin said, "I knew, but I didn't think anyone else did."

Missing first base doesn't just happen on the baseball field; it happens in everyday life. Finding intimacy with God requires touching first base. One must first receive Jesus Christ as their personal Savior by believing and trusting in Him to find everlasting peace with God. This must contain a repentant heart before God.

Touching first base grants the believer an opportunity to enjoy peace *with* God—no more conflicts and separation. However, the peace *of* God is found when a believer truly follows Jesus and makes Him Lord and Master over their life. By remaining close to Jesus one can find rest within and have victory over daily sin.

The Apostle Paul, in the Bible, declared to us believers and followers of Jesus that there was another peace offered to us. This peace is identified in scripture as the peace *of* God, which is different. This peace *of* God enables us to cease from all worrying regardless of our circumstances. Relinquishing our concerns and petitions over to God in prayer with our deepest gratitude will result in amazing personal outcomes.

Paul writes and says that the peace *of* God, which is so far beyond our human comprehension, will shelter and protect our whole person as we remain in followship with our Lord Jesus Christ. This newly recognized peace *of* God, that I did not understand at all, enabled me to find the coping mechanism to alleviate my need for alcohol. The peace *of* God is real and available to each one of us.

For me, there was no joining in the twelve steps of Alcoholics Anonymous or any other program but simply abiding in Christ. It was the peace *with* and *of* God that replaced my need to seek the numbness of life found in alcohol.

The key to enjoying this ongoing peace of God is found in Jesus's own words:

> "If you abide in Me, and My words abide in you, ask whatever you wish, and it will be done for you." John 15:7 (NASB)

Abiding in Christ points a believer toward seeking intimacy with our heavenly Father. This will ultimately develop into a lifelong passion since chasing intimacy continuously provides deep spiritual satisfaction and worry-free living.

> "Do not worry about anything, but in everything by prayer and supplication with thanksgiving let your requests be made known to God. And the peace of God, which surpasses all understanding, will guard your hearts and your minds in Christ Jesus." Philippians 4:6–7 (NRSV)

CHAPTER 20

Coping with Tragedies

Prior to finding peace *with* God and the peace *of* God in my life, I was a drunk, not a mean drunk, but a happy drunk! My sense of humor was released when drinking, and my friends all wanted me to resume my role as the life of the party. Often upon arrival after greeting all my bar mates, my fate would be prearranged. Awaiting at my customary bar seat would be four double rum and cokes—compliments of my friends.

My normal practice was to drink three down almost nonstop and then take the fourth in my hand and begin sipping it more sociably. Getting drunk was a routine procedure, which often led me to memory blackouts and the additional danger of driving thirty-five miles home to Ortonville. Oh yeah, before I drove home, it was my usual practice to head over to a nearby restaurant, that was owned by my good friend, in the early morning hours to eat a big breakfast and drink lots of coffee allowing time to enable me back into soberness.

Even my closest friends were glad after I quit drinking for fear of driving so far home. However, they were not very happy that I had found Christ to be my answer, and they completely rejected my new walk of faith. One of my closest friends, Mike, defended me for quite some time and remained a close friend after my salvation experience, but he also finally walked away from me.

Often Mike and I would spend time fishing together and he would ask a lot of questions about my newfound faith.

I finally said, "Mike, what prevents you from receiving Christ as your Savior?"

He told me that he was not ready to make that step. At that time, he was living with a girl outside of marriage and for him to make such a decision would mean his life would have to change. He did not want to marry this girl or marry anyone because of his parent's previous bitter divorce. He just said no thanks to God's offer. I still pray for Mike.

My excuse—and most drunks have one tucked away somewhere—was dealing with the terrible situations witnessed firsthand as a cop. Controlling my feelings was a legitimate concern, but drunkenness was not the right answer.

A police call was given out that a child was choking. Being a one-man unit and close to the address, I responded to the call within thirty seconds. Entering the house, the mother was kneeling over a two-year-old child in the bathroom. She was attempting to administer mouth-to-mouth resuscitation, but her son's head was tilted forward, thereby closing off the airway. I pushed her aside, immediately cleared the airway, and began correct mouth-to-mouth resuscitation. The ambulance arrived, and the attendants rushed the child out to the ambulance and placed him on an inhalator and sped off to the hospital. The house was dimly lit, and everything had moved very quickly.

After my inquiries at the scene, I drove to Beaumont Hospital to complete my incident report. As I was writing my report, the lead doctor came into the room and asked me to follow him. Upon entering the examining room, there were several tables with large bright lights over each. One of the tables had the stretched out little body of the child.

The doctor asked me if I had a chance to examine this child at the scene.

I explained that everything had happened very quickly and that I did not really look closely at the child. He escorted me up to the examining table, and I stood directly over the lifeless body of this two-year old boy.

The doctor pointed out the marks all over the child's body. I could plainly see that they were human teeth marks. He pulled on the upper lip of the child and showed me how the lip had been split all the back to the nose. He grabbed my hand and pressed it into the abdominal area of the child. He said, "Do you feel that lump?"

I said, "Yes."

He moved my hand to another location and repeated the question.

I felt another clump of tissue.

He then placed my hand on a third location and repeated the question.

I said, "Yes. I feel that."

He said, "Officer, this child has been beaten to death!"

I contacted my command sergeant and shared this newly revealed information. A short time later we arrested both parents for murder. The picture of that child shall never leave my memory bank. Large amounts of consumed alcohol helped dim that picture and provide some temporary relief from the disparagement of that scene.

The court proceedings, with murder charges levied against both parents, unraveled with the father turning state's evidence to avoid prosecution and testifying against his wife. She informed the court that she had lost control of herself due to the child being sick and crying all the time. Things changed when the defense attorney permitted the jury to view the photos of the child that we took at the hospital, and that ultimately resulted in a guilty verdict. The mother was convicted of third-degree murder (manslaughter) and was sentenced from one to fifteen years in prison. She was paroled in six months, and there was no psychological help required for her.

The entire case made me disgusted inside. I thought about the many inadequacies in the due process of law. Was it fair to that little child—and was justice really done? I presume that this question could likewise be asked on behalf of an aborted child just prior to birth. Bewildered? Yes! Drinking helped me cope as any drug (legal or illegal) might do; however, the turmoil remained unresolved and firmly wedged in my memory bank.

Another vivid reminder was of a fifteen-year-old boy who had taken a .22 caliber rifle, placed the tip of the barrel to his chest, and discharged a round right through his heart in a fit of anger against a society that was crushing in around him. The teenager's body was stretched out on top of a heap of garbage in their dining room. The family lived like animals. The frustration in this teen's life was certainly validated, and he was swept into the grave by ending his life. So young to die! And yes, maybe just a few more drinks would help me forget.

Recalling a young woman found lying face down in the garage who had decided to end her life by taking rat poison. I turned over her body, and the rat poison had eaten away a portion of the right side of her face. Just another day on the job, but it added another tragic end to a precious life and another entry into my memory bank.

I went on a call to the scene of a family disturbance. The woman screamed at us that he was in the bedroom. As we approached the room, we heard a shotgun blast. This man had placed a .12-gauge shotgun to this head and literally scattered his brains all over the wall. No more hope of reconciliation for this couple—and another picture of real life to scramble my psyche.

At seven o'clock on a Sunday morning, I was dispatched to the scene of a multiple car accident. One vehicle was so badly mangled and crushed that in the back seat, all I could see was arms, legs, and heads, but I could not tell which arm or leg belonged to which body. There were three people crushed in the back of this car. Two were fatalities and a twenty-three-year-old girl was transformed into a paraplegic for the rest of her life. This family was on their way to church on a quiet Sunday morning.

Dear reader, I am sorry that you should even picture any of these things in your mind, but my point is to share with you that this is real life. Not knowing how to personally cope with these tragedies at that time became my excuse. When drunk and happy, there was some relief; however, there were no solutions.

Reading about these kinds of incidents in the newspaper or seeing blurbs on the news is not the same as seeing them firsthand and up close. Yes, alcohol did help me cope. It was my only legal remedy to find some type of peace in this bewildering and harsh world that I was currently existing in. Was booze going to be my only help through these tragedies? And, how did I, as a matter of fact, get started walking down this road of insobriety?

CHAPTER 21

Booze Beginnings

It always seems to start off very innocently. After joining the police department, I was assigned to a specific uniformed shift. The officers were a very tight and exclusive group. To fit in, one must prove himself to be a trustworthy, reliable, and fraternal brother. Cops often depended upon one another for their very lives. Of course, I wanted to fit in with my fellow police officers and this required submission to their standards.

Around the end of the first month of my rookie days, the guys invited me to a card game. They would occasionally get together after work to have a few beers and play some cards. Refusing wasn't an option since I desired to fit in and wanted to be accepted. Isn't that true of all of us? Even in elementary school and especially through high school all one craved was to be part of the group.

It is a proven fact that people will even do wrong to be accepted into a group, which is often found in gang mentality. It is easy to understand why young people in high school and college go to parties, drink large amounts of alcohol, and even take drugs because their peers are all doing it. The military, workplaces, and youth and church groups provide that same type of camaraderie.

The group influence can be good or bad, depending upon the leadership of the group. For me, one beer led to another, then another, and then fast-forwarding into habitual drinking.

Christmas morning in 1966 was one such event. Our shift had completed its tour of duty at seven o'clock. It was my first time working a Christmas Eve shift. It had been a reasonably quiet and cold evening in the city. One event that was rippling through my memory was a call to a family fight at two o'clock in the morning. Yes, a family fight on early Christmas Day morning!

As my partner, Stan, and I approached the front of the house, we heard screaming and yelling inside. We cautiously walked up to the front porch. As we got to the door, a glittering, flashing Christmas tree—complete with all the trimmings—came crashing through the front plate glass window. Glass exploded everywhere, and the arguing spouses were screaming at one another and running through the house.

We entered the house and began to chase after them. The husband was standing in the hallway with a bat in his hands. We drew our sidearms and proceeded to disarm him. We put them both on the couch and began to talk with them. He was angry because she wasn't ready to go out to a dinner party when he got home from work. Of course, he was half-filled to the gills from an office party he had just left and was four hours late for the dinner party. She was ticked off and went to bed. "Have yourself a merry little Christmas," were not the melodic sounds heard in that household!

At the close of our shift, I learned that it was a yearly Christmas custom for some local businessmen to provide a Texas-sized fifth of whiskey for the police officers to enjoy after duty hours. The whiskey, soda, glasses, and ice were placed on the ping-pong table in the basement locker room. Our shift was dismissed from our tour of duty at seven o'clock.

Our sergeant said, "Merry Christmas!"

All the men then went down to the locker room to change clothes and put their gear away. Some of the officers went out the back door and headed directly home to be with their families on Christmas morning. I went down to my locker to put away all my stuff and retrieve my off-duty Colt .38 snub-nosed revolver.

Terri and I were new parents with our son Jeff, who was three months old. It was our first Christmas with our newborn, and we were both very excited. Our plans were to have our own gift exchange in the morning when I got home. Then after a few hours of sleep, we would go over to visit her mom and then head over to my mom and dad's house in Madison Heights for our annual Christmas dinner.

As I was walking out of the station, a fellow officer said, "Hey, Al, aren't you going to have one drink with us before you go home?"

I thought, *I don't want a drink. My stomach is still queasy from all the coffee, greasy food, and holiday treats I consumed all night long.*

"No thanks," I said. "Merry Christmas."

"Aw, come on Al, just one," another cop said.

I said, "Well, guys, I promised my wife that I would be home right after the shift is over."

By then, more of the men were standing around the ping-pong table and pouring whiskey into glasses of ice. They shoved a glass of whiskey into my hand.

One of them said, "Come on, Al. Just have one with the guys."

I knew what that meant. If I refused, it meant that I wouldn't be accepted as one of the guys. So, I stepped back into the room. We all sat around with our drinks and talked about the events we encountered during the past week.

Our shift proudly considered itself to be the "cleanup" shift. There was a certain pride and camaraderie on each shift, and they pulled together as a team. We prided ourselves as the shift that made the most felony arrests when we moved to the midnight rotation, cleaning up the city. We were very aggressive as a shift and truly looked out for one another. There is a fraternal bonding—like the military in battle—when our lives are put on the line. The most important call we would ever respond to with absolute quickness was a dispatch of an "officer in trouble." That was the ultimate priority in policework, and the second highest priority was dispatches involving children.

I finished my drink as we talked about observing the flying Christmas tree through the window and dealing with the real-life Scrooge at the house.

One of the men commented about his ex-wife with a few expletives and summarized his Christmas by saying, "Bah, humbug!"

We all laughed, and I got up to leave. I started for the door as several of the guys were exiting through the back door. Five men were standing around the basement door.

"Al, come on back here! I need to ask you a question," said one of my fellow officers.

I stepped back into the room, and another drink was handed to me.

I said, "No, but thanks, guys. I really have to get home."

They chuckled, "Yeah, so do we—but just one more for the road."

By then, I started to feel the warming effects of the whiskey swirling through my body. Drinking was not my thing, as I absolutely disliked the taste of whiskey and beer.

"One more," they said.

We were all starting to feel the effects of the booze. My strength was beginning to turn into weakness as the peer pressure continued. The fraternal bonding seemed to increase as we continued to drink away the entire Texas fifth.

Stan, Denny, Ron, and I were the only ones left. Stan had been going through difficulties in his marriage and really didn't want to go home. Denny—affectionately nicknamed Barney Fife—was my best friend on the police department since we were hired on the same day. We became best friends during the academy and throughout most of my police career. We spent many days up north (a term used for northern Michigan) together hunting, fishing, trail riding, snowmobiling, building his cabin in Glennie, MI and spending many hours barhopping the area. He was, in my opinion, the real life of the party and had the funniest sense of humor of anyone I ever knew. The more we drank, the funnier things got. Ron, Denny, and I all knew that we needed to get home, but the influence of the whiskey subsequently diminished our allegiance to our families as it swirled through our brains.

Ron said, "Let's go over to my place and have a Christmas drink. My wife will make us some breakfast."

It sounded like a good idea, and we all drove over to Ron's house. We sat at his breakfast table on Christmas morning, drank some more, and ate breakfast. His wife, Mary, tried to be cordial with us and made us breakfast. She was quite upset since she had Christmas plans with Ron and their kids, but what was she to do? She kind of grinned to bear it as we joked with her and their kids. At around noon, we parted company, hugging one another in a semi-drunken stupor and wishing one another slurred Christmas greetings.

Arriving at home a little before noon, I was barely able to stand up. Mary had called Terri to let her know that I was still alive and told her what had happened that morning. In my drunken stupor—and trying to be joyful when arriving at home—I began wishing Terri "Happy Christmas" greetings. She seemed to be handling it OK while I stumbled into our bedroom and removed my clothes for sleep. Little did I know that she was really ticked off as I dozed off with my brain still swirling from all the intoxicants.

Terri decided to wake me in three hours to go to my parents no matter how I was feeling. Three hours later, she followed through with her plan and even poured water on my head to wake me up. Feeling incredibly miserable, I did get up. My head was spinning and pounding with that sick feeling all over.

After showering, we drove over to my folks' house. I remembered very little of that Christmas day other than feeling miserable throughout the entire afternoon and evening.

Yes, my motivation was to fit in with my fellow police officers, but little did I know that those early booze beginnings would lead me into a downward spiral. Alcohol became my crutch, leading me to a separation from Terri and nearly a divorce. Very little time with our children, compounding financial woes, and thousands of wasted dollars on bar tabs nearly led us to bankruptcy. During those dark times, my life was sidetracked from finding any genuine peace. I sensed that I was being held in the grip of sin and remained empty inside. I needed to be set free.

CHAPTER 22

Rookie Acceptance

Rotating shifts was a monthly occurrence. One month, my patrol shift would be assigned midnights (11:00 p.m. to 7:00 a.m.), then we would rotate to the afternoon shift (3:00 p.m. to 11:00 p.m.) for a month, and then we would be assigned a day shift (7:00 a.m. to 3:00 p.m.). Rookies had to prove themselves in the line of duty before they were fully accepted by the rest of the officers. There was a traditional proving ground that must take place before a rookie is truly accepted as a fellow officer. When danger presents itself to a rookie cop, he must prove himself reliable and trustworthy to his fellow officers. For each patrolman, the situation would vary, and each rookie might have a different set of testing circumstances. Mine occurred on a day shift about two months after I was hired.

My assignment was to ride with senior Officer Bill Borland that day. We were dispatched to the scene of a man threatening his wife. We arrived at the scene and entered the house. The husband was sitting on the couch when we entered the living room after being invited in by the wife. She told us that her husband no longer lived at that house and that he was asked to leave. The house belonged to her mother, and the wife was separated from her husband. They had one child, and the husband came over to visit the child, but he was no longer welcome to stay there and wouldn't leave.

Officer Borland called the owner of the house, and she told us to throw him out because he did not belong there. We walked over to the man and informed him that he had to leave. We could smell strong intoxicants on his breath.

He looked up at us and shouted, "You (expletives deleted) cops are never going to take me out of this house!"

I looked at Bill, an experienced officer, and he looked at me. He told the man to leave again, but he refused to acknowledge the warning.

The third time Bill announced that he must leave, after trying to reason with him some more, the man's voice became even louder with his declaration that we "pigs" were not going to take him anywhere. He was a tough looking, muscularly built construction worker, and he had been using marijuana along with some other drugs. On top of that, he had been drinking for the past two days because he had lost his job.

Bill had given him three warnings, and there was no more to be said. Bill told him he was going to jail if we had to escort him out of the house.

He challenged us with a haughty laugh and said, "You pigs aren't taking me anywhere!"

Bill removed his hat and set it on the buffet.

As rookies, we were informed to keep our mouths shut and do whatever our senior partners did. So, I placed my hat next to Bill's.

Bill grabbed his left side, and I grabbed his right side, but he didn't move. This guy was not going to be easy; he was solid muscle. We attempted to place him in handcuffs.

We struggled and fought with him for nearly twenty minutes and destroyed a good portion of the entire living room. The TV was busted, furniture was broken, lamps were smashed, and the couch was turned upside down. I finally got one arm pinned behind his back, and Bill was holding the other arm under his leg.

I was able to get his one wrist cuffed, but we struggled for another ten minutes to get them handcuffed together. He was one of the toughest men I had ever encountered, but we succeeded in finally getting our now prisoner out to the back of the squad car. My uniform shirt was torn almost off, and Bill's was ripped along with his pants. We booked him at the station, and another struggle occurred trying to get him into his cell. We were both physically exhausted from the series of events that day, but the mission had been accomplished.

The word spread like wildfire through the police station that I had proven myself under fire. Now officially accepted as a brother officer, the attitude of my fellow cops changed toward me completely. They now knew that I could handle myself under pressure and be counted trustworthy as a fellow patrolman. The unofficial nod of approval had been given to me as one fully accepted.

Another incident enabling my confirmation occurred on a day shift. It was a lazy, warm summer day. Royal Oak in the 1970s was a city of about eighty-five thousand people with a dying downtown business district. A shortage of parking and a new shopping mall in Troy were some of the reasons for the decline.

The Grand Trunk Railroad passed directly through the heart of the downtown area. A long train was able to divide the west side from the east side of the city for a duration of time while passing through the city. Quite often, a long and loaded southbound train would exceed the railway speed of thirty-five miles per hour through town. The trains usually had so many cars that nobody seemed to care about the train's speed since the intersections in town were blocked for more than the maximum limit of five minutes. People would often get very irritated while waiting for these long trains to pass through town.

A seventeen-year-old girl was walking South on Washington Avenue. She had passed by the post office and sauntered toward the downtown business district. As she approached the railroad crossing, she appeared undaunted by the noises of an oncoming train sounding off its horn in the distance. The crossing gates came down to block the flow of all traffic, and the crossing lights began to flash red. The bells began to ring loudly, signifying the warning of a train. The young girl continued to stroll almost as if she was in a trance.

The loud wail of the diesel's horn alerted everyone within a mile radius, and the train was moving very quickly. It was one of those southbound trains with over a mile of railway cars attached. The horn blared additional warnings as the train moved at a higher rate of speed through town.

As the train approached the intersection at Washington Avenue, the engineer who sat on the front right of the diesel engine observed the girl walking toward the tracks. He thought she would stop, but she continued walking as if in a daydream. The engineer sounded the horn again and again to get her attention, but he had to watch her young life step directly into the pathway of that train. Her last movement was to look up—as if being awakened from sleep—with a surprised expression. It was over quickly. She dropped underneath the big steel wheels of that huge diesel engine, tumbling, and turning her body for a quarter of a mile. An emergency stop was enacted by the train, but it took more than a mile to finally halt that monstrosity.

My assignment that day was to a downtown area beat. The call was dispatched to me, and I was not very far from the scene. Upon arrival, the entire train had come to a stop, and the caboose ended up more than half a mile away from the accident location. People began to mill about as the fire department, ambulances, and other emergency vehicles began to arrive.

The conductor of the train walked all the way back from the caboose and approached me. He was white-faced and breathing quite hard. "Officer, she was just a young girl." He pointed to a clump about five hundred feet down the tracks.

Some firemen and I ran down to where the girl's body was located. Her body was severally mangled. Her legs were both severed just below her knees, and there was exposed muscle and bone. We found several body parts and placed them in plastic bags. There were even some of her brains on the ground near the scene of the impact.

The engineer and brakeman who rode in the front of the train finally arrived from their long walk back to the intersection. The brakeman told me that he had observed the girl walking toward the crossing. The loud diesel horn was sounding as she stepped into the pathway of the train. Just before the impact, she opened her eyes like she had just awakened from a sound sleep, but it was too late.

I interviewed the other witnesses at the scene, and everyone corroborated the brakeman's story. Her body was removed after measurements and photographs were taken. The train was permitted to continue its journey, and the brakeman and the engineer walked away with profound sadness on their faces.

After completing my reports at the scene, I went to Beaumont Hospital to finish up my incident report. After three hours of overtime, I finally returned to the station.

Lieutenant Wells, the afternoon shift commander, was sitting at his desk as I turned in all my reports for his review. He thoroughly examined my reports and stacked them all neatly together as I waited for his approval and my tour of duty release. He informed me that I had done a very good job. It made me feel good that he recognized all my efforts, extensive report, and thoroughness. My peers soon heard of my well-done piece of policework. The word spread rapidly. He told me that I could head home, and after thanking him, I started to walk away from the front desk.

Starting down the stairs to my locker, the lieutenant shouted, "Hey, Novak!"

I stopped and walked back to his desk.

He said, "By the way, pardner, you have to be at the autopsy at eight o'clock tomorrow morning." It was the state law at the time that the investigating officer was to be present so that the pathologist could have positive identification of the body and answer any questions. I thought sarcastically, *What a great way to start a Sunday morning!*

CHAPTER 23

The Human Body

I had to get up extra early the next morning to arrive at Beaumont Hospital on time. We lived in Ortonville, which was about thirty-seven miles from Royal Oak. As I drove in, all I could think about was observing my first autopsy!

The pathology unit was in the lower portion of the hospital. Dr. Greer was performing the autopsy. He asked if I had witnessed an autopsy before.

I shook my head negatively.

He escorted me into the examination room. There was a wall of refrigerated drawers each about three feet square. He told me that I would learn a lot about human anatomy during the autopsy, and he would explain each procedure before he began. He also noted that if I had a squeamish stomach along the way, that it would be OK if I stepped out of the room.

I told him that I had seen worse on the street already, recalling yesterday's scene, and perhaps it was too late to be squeamish.

He pulled open drawer number ten. As the body rolled out headfirst, he transferred the cadaver to the examining table and turned on some extremely bright overhead lights. A foot pedal controlled a tape-recording unit in which the doctor, describing things in medical terms, verbally defined each procedure.

The body was completely visible and facing up. He asked me, for the record, if I recognized the body as the same one that I had observed at the scene of the train accident yesterday.

I answered in the affirmative. He began to describe the overall cadaver. He stated that she was seventeen years old and obese.

I thought, *This girl isn't obese. She may have been a few pounds overweight, but I certainly wouldn't describe her as obese.*

The next procedure (by the way if you have a weak or squeamish stomach, you may want to skip through this part since it is quite descriptive) was to take a scalpel and cut from the neck down to the abdomen. I started to get a little bit queasy, but I swallowed and moved one step back. As the incision was made, it seemed like the skin began to bloat. It looked like it was being inflated. That was the first time I had visually observed body fat under the skin line. She had about an inch or more of excessive fat. *Maybe the doctor was right about being obese*, I thought. *What about my body? What's under my skin line? He probably would describe me as super obese since I'm around forty pounds overweight. I always called myself simply "big framed", ha!*

The doctor began to remove the organs, one at a time, and described them using medical terminology that I did not fully understand. He would cut a few pieces from each organ and place them into separate jars of formaldehyde, always stopping and showing me each organ. This was the first time I had observed a human heart, lung, or kidney. My interest continued to increase in the identification process, and I began to move closer to the body while observing. He finished his discourse, placed all the organs together in a plastic bag, and inserted them into the chest cavity.

He then proceeded with a surgical cut from ear to ear at the base of the skull. Pulling the skin over the head, he tucked it under the chin, exposing the skull area. I had heard of suffering with a fractured skull injury before, but I had never seen one up close. It looked like a broken skull bone puzzle with fractures in many places. He removed the pieces carefully, removed the entire brain, and placed it on a scale.

A puzzled look came over him as he began to describe the weight and description of the brain. Something was wrong; the brain was not the normal size for a person of this age. He stopped in a moment of bewilderment.

I said, "Doc, does something seem wrong?"

He said, "Yes, this brain is about five to ten ounces shy of the expected normal weight."

I told him that I had found small clumps of brains while I was searching along the tracks. The impact and tumbling under the train had literally forced brains out of her head.

The doctor expressed how thankful he was for that information. It solved a real puzzle for him. Just then an intern doctor walked into the pathology room, and Dr. Greer began to holler loudly at him and ordered him to get out. The outburst from the seemingly mild-mannered doctor kind of unnerved me. After the intern left, the doctor explained the reason for his actions.

He said that he hollered at him to divert his attention away from the cadaver. He previously had interns walk in during the middle of a procedure and be so shocked that they would leave the medical profession. He never allowed anyone to enter his area during a procedure because of that shock factor.

I was relieved to hear that, and I thought, *I am not even a medical student, and I am witnessing the whole autopsy standing right next to the doctor.* My self-esteem began to pump up as I thought about my accomplishments that day.

After Dr. Greer finished, he dismissed me. I signed the

necessary papers as a witness and left the hospital. Years later, after continually witnessing tragic events during my police career, a developed unrest remained constantly nagging at my heart. This turmoil in my spirit had me living without any peace at all. I was hungering for some genuine quietude within. It wasn't until ten years later—after receiving Christ as my personal Savior—that my circumstances improved.

While reading Philippians 4:6–7, I discovered that God designed a plan for us to handle these day-to-day struggles, and it wasn't with alcohol or drugs. His plan was also known as the peace *of* God, and it is available for each one of us.

Experiencing peace *with* God begins by faith and trust in Jesus Christ. Enjoying the peace *of* God begins when allowing Jesus to be Lord over your life. The definition of life eternal and intimacy with God is included in Jesus' prayer found John's gospel:

> "This is eternal life, that they may know You, the only true God, and Jesus Christ whom You have sent." John 17:3 (NASB)

Thomas, an apostle of Jesus, had asked Him a few chapters previously:

> "...and how can we know the way? Jesus said to him, 'I am the way, the truth, and the life. No one comes to the Father except through Me.'" John 14:5–6 (NKJV)

Knowing God is eternal life and is only applicable when, by faith, one believes and receives Jesus as their personal Savior. This initial step of faith then allows us to get acquainted with the only true God and pursue an intimate relationship with Him. Chasing intimacy can become the most satisfying part of one's faith walk.

Imagine (picture) yourself sitting in God's lap as His precious little child and sensing His loving arms around you, holding you tightly. Your Heavenly Father really loves you!

> "He who does not love does not know God, for God is love." 1 John 4:8 (NKJV)

CHAPTER 24

Bloom Where You Are Planted!

It was around my eleventh year on the PD that I became a Christian. My life changed completely. Randy continued to disciple me for several years since I had many spiritual questions to resolve. My Roman Catholic background left me with many puzzling questions about traditional Catholic teachings and biblical doctrine. I finally determined that regardless of the teaching, if it was found written in the Bible and supported contextually, that my adherence would be to the apostles' teachings. My practice of "Solo Scriptura" (scripture alone) became one of my tenets as was taught by the reformer, Martin Luther, in the 1500s.

Terri and I agreed that in many locations, the scriptures did not line up with what we were taught or not taught as Catholics. We began to search for a new church family. We attended several Lutheran churches, finally landing at Christ Missouri Synod Evangelical Lutheran Church in Hadley, Michigan. We were part of that family for several years, and we grew to love the pastor and the church family.

We embraced Martin Luther's Solo Fide (faith alone), Sola Scriptura (scripture alone), Sola Gratia (grace alone), Soli Deo Gloria (glory to God alone), and added a clear step of departure from Catholic teaching that genuine salvation is found in Solus Christus (Christ alone). Our spiritual lives were totally reformed.

After several more years of bible study, Terri and I determined that we had issues with the Lutheran teachings related to consubstantiation and infant baptism. Sadly, we departed from our Lutheran church family. Subsequently, we joined Ortonville Baptist Church and remained there in fellowship for seven years. Previously while searching for a church home, we listed any church except Baptist. I predetermined without research that this denomination was closely linked to the KKK, which I wanted no part of. This may be true of some Baptist churches down South, but it was not true in Ortonville, MI.

We heard the clear preaching of the Bible (the Word of God) every Sunday at Ortonville Baptist Church. We grew to love the entire church family. We also learned to appreciate the older hymns of faith as they truly ministered to our hearts. The folks there became like family to us. Pastor Bill Bronkema was our spiritual leader, and he was a very kind person and exuberant preacher. God allowed me to serve as a deacon for six years in that leadership role. Our church family was devoted to the Word of God and fellowship with other believers, and we had lots of great times there.

This was also the beginning years of my sliding into legalism and my indoctrination into unacceptance and condemnation of other believers. Our church was in fellowship with the General Association of Regular Baptists, a group that ultimately became separatists in the name of God. I found that many leaders in that association were nitpickers and disapproved of other true believers who also were preaching Christ.

A significant factor in this book, revealing my journey of faith, began with an intimate personal cry to God. Denominational barriers were being set in place that found us slipping into legalism within the church. This part of my story contains some of those breakthrough years of unmasking this legalism and judgmentalism and rediscovering that my deepest desire was indeed seeking intimacy with God.

Learning more about God and Jesus through the preaching and teaching of the Word greatly encouraged us—and so did the great old hymns of the faith that we heard—but deep within my heart I still longed for more of Him. It is not what you know about the Bible that changes your life; it is how well you know the God of the Bible (John 17:3). This is what really changes a person!

After several more years of studying the Word, I began to sense God's leading toward full-time Christian service. Church missionaries would come and go at different times and present glowing reports to the church of what God was doing in their mission field. I began to pray to God about sending us into missions. I would nudge Terri and say, "How about going to Bolivia or into some other foreign overseas mission that we would hear about?"

She would politely tell me that she really liked Michigan.

I figured that if God wanted me in foreign missions, He would have to convince her also. "Michigan? Where would there be any missions in Michigan?"

I heard a missionary once say that only 15 percent of the people living in Michigan were evangelized. Thinking about all the people I knew who were truly born-again believers gave that statistic considerable validity.

After hearing from so many of the missionaries, I found myself constantly praying to God about serving Him somewhere in the mission field.

With foreign missions still swirling in my brain, I was assigned that day to my beat assignment as a one-man unit. Often when alone and praying aloud to God, I enjoyed some special times of intimacy with Him.

For some reason that day, I stopped my squad car and shoved my hand into the crease of the front bench seat to see what might be stuck down in there. Occasionally I found things like a pen, or coins, or miscellaneous items from time to time that were stuck in-between the seat. On this occasion I pulled out a glossy colored brochure that had been crushed into the crease of the seat. After flattening it out, it displayed a beautiful picture of a brightly colored flower. The words boldly written under the flower said, "Bloom Where You are Planted."

Wow, I knew that God was speaking directly to me at that moment. Rather than going somewhere else to find a mission field, God informed me that my mission field was right there on the police department—and with everyone I would meet along the way. God wanted and needed me right there!

My answer was, "Yes, Lord! I will do whatever you ask of me." Every situation now presented itself as an opportunity to share Jesus with whomever I met. Fellow officers, those I arrested, the victims of crime and mayhem, and the homeless downtrodden were all viewed differently now. All the people in Royal Oak, as opportunity presented itself, became my mission field. God answered my continual request for missions with a simple, "Bloom Where You are Planted." He wasn't looking for my skill, but my availability only.

Randy and I were asked by our public safety director to start an in-house police chaplaincy program, and we did. Many of our fellow officers were reluctant and ridiculed us, but a few came to know the Lord as their Savior. After family disturbance calls, additional time was permitted to share Jesus with the combatants at the scene. It always amazed me that I never would get a call back from those who prayed with me to receive Christ as their Savior.

What a privilege to be used by God and to witness Him transform lives. All it took was being available to Him wherever I was! To God be the glory and honor! Amen.

Of course, common sense for the *chaplainized* police officers were always required, especially when taking time to share Christ with others. The duties and responsibilities of police work always came first and foremost, and it was only when opportunities presented themselves during certain calls that time was taken to share our faith with others along the way. Our goals were always to resolve the trouble at the scene. I would pray over those who would listen and then add them to my daily prayer list.

Common sense and Christian sense partnered together in our police chaplaincy endeavors. I recall another incident during a day shift that we received a dispatch to a house where a man had shot and killed another man and wounded another person with a high-powered rifle. He had barricaded himself in the house.

As officers situated themselves behind cover and surrounded the house, our handheld "pep" radios were blurting out all sorts of information.

One of my fellow officers aired, "Hey, is Novak here?"

Someone else said, "Yeah, he is on the east side of the house."

"Well, since he is one of them so-called chaplains, have him go up on the front porch and talk to this guy!"

The radio clicked several times from those agreeing in a mockingly and ridiculing manner, but common sense of course prevailed. I remained silent behind a tree and denied their request, but I was praying intently over the seriousness of the incident. After quite some time of negotiations and waiting it out, the assailant finally gave himself up.

Most of the officers were nice guys and honorable, but they were just nonbelievers. Spiritual matters that were not understood simply became suspect to them. The process of sharing Christ with our fellow officers was very slow-moving and often barren of any fruit. I found myself being tested just prior to our police line-ups. My fellow officers took great pleasure in loudly vocalizing filthy and explicit and sinful stories just to watch my response.

They would laugh in my face, and I would put my head down, in an aura of deep shame. I was sad for our Lord who had died for these men. I learned that it was best to just remain down in the locker room until the very last minute before lineup began to avoid these spiritually uncomfortable situations. After all, wisdom is God's perspective on everything, as Jesus said:

> "See, I am sending you out like sheep into the midst of wolves; so be wise as serpents and innocent as doves." Matthew 10:16 (NRSV)

CHAPTER 25

Sliding into Legalism

As a new believer, it is normal to think that all Christians are the same. You know, one big happy family. Well, to my dismay, I soon discovered that there are many differences in Christian teachings and between believers, which sometimes leads to animosity. Denominational differences were exposed and camped upon, especially within churches that claimed to be fundamental. It seemed that the formal Orthodox Christian churches were more unwavering in their teachings and remained steadfast with the same rituals offered at every service.

Legalism was certainly a downer for the Christian movement, and it was practiced everywhere. Certain degrees of separation were even suggested for fellow Christian believers. Some taught first-degree separation, which is choosing to separate and have nothing to do with those who practice or support certain doctrines. The second-degree separationists separated from those who associated with those of a different doctrine or practice. Some even moved into third- or fourth-degree disassociation.

Dear Lord, what nonsense you must endure with those trying to share Jesus in this lost and dying world, I thought. *Didn't Jesus pray in John 17 that we might be one as He is one with His Father?* Well, legalism certainly drove—and continues to drive—a wedge into His prayer request for unity among His followers. When trying to fit in with fellow believers, it is easy to get caught up into legalism and point the finger of heresy toward other believers. We can disagree on interpretations but shouldn't be disagreeable with our fellow believers. *Oh, Lord Jesus, give us a deeper understanding of Your heart cry for unity!*

There are doctrinal differences shared among Christians but rejecting and shunning genuine believers who love Jesus Christ with unkind remarks is wrong. This can be assigned as the *sin of dogmatism*. Determining that one is totally correct in their doctrinal position is a real form of pride and know-it-all-ism. It is the I-am-right-and-you-are-wrong complex. It is declaring that I am the teacher of all truth and that you should just be the acknowledging student. Shouldn't we all just be students of the Word and seekers of truth?

The most hurtful word ever delivered from a fellow believer's lips against another believer, in my opinion, is the word, *heretic*. That word accuses other believers of false teaching and declares with a prideful attitude their possession of the absolute and final truth. The word *heretic* is often bounced around among the jargon of legalists. May we all be reminded that Jesus said He was the truth, and I believe that He alone is exactly that. Apart from there being only one true God and His only begotten Son, Jesus Christ, His Messiah, and our Redeemer, we can debate almost every teaching and find some supportable differences. It doesn't free us from being kind to one another, does it?

The legalists argue, "We must reject them completely!"

1. Billy Graham, the greatest evangelist of our time, had a Catholic bishop on his platform. Let's reject him.

2. He wore a "Jesus First" lapel pin. Let's reject him.
3. Those believers in Jesus spoke in tongues. Let's reject them.
4. They baptize infants with sprinkling. Let's reject them.
5. They baptize only in the name of Jesus. Let's reject them.
6. They do not use the King James Bible. Let's reject them.
7. They sing contemporary Christian music. Let's reject them.
8. It goes on and on, leading into *"taedium vitae"* (look it up).

The legalists' ongoing cry is, "Burn them at the stake. Heretics!" I was caught up in legalism and thinking that I was always right. Shame on me. Shame on them. Shame on us!

During those introductory years to the Christian life, there were many decisions that we made, especially in training up our first three children. Jeff, Mike, and Jenni were taught a lot of good moral stuff, but we were also teaching them to be good little legalists as they grew up—just like we had become. We disassociated and looked down on other fellow believers who played cards, drank alcoholic beverages (a.k.a. sippin' saints), attended movies, or enjoyed dancing. This also included many shouting arguments with my older brothers and parents who were deeply indoctrinated into Catholicism and it's traditions.

After a while, we avoided talking about spiritual matters during all our family gatherings since they only ended in contention. Again, disagreeing and being disagreeable must be bathed in love and kindness. The followship of Jesus requires us to seek unity. Shame on those believers who continue to practice legalism and remain committed to abiding in the sin of dogmatism! My friend, this sin is still widely practiced among believers today.

Thank You Lord for this reminder that we should always be kind to one another especially in the discussion of religion and politics as we often have differences of opinion. Amen.

The truth will be known when Jesus returns since He declared Himself to be the truth.

CHAPTER 26

Career Change

After much family discussion—and thoughts and plans—a decision was made to resign from my police career. After seventeen years as a police officer, in good standing with the city of Royal Oak, I submitted my resignation. A new career in the service industry was looming in our future. With glowing anticipation of this new adventure, Terri and I entered the restaurant business.

Financially, we put everything on the line. We promoted our new business as a family friendly American cuisine restaurant with a touch of class. In addition, we leased rows of standing video games for young people to play, which were visible from the dining area. A self-playing ragtime piano along with a 1920s motif that included handmade tiffany lamps over each table was our prototype design. Our restaurant was named "The Scoring 20's."

It was a great idea with great potential. We had home-made-style food with a touch of class, but we later discovered that we inadvertently selected the wrong location. We established our restaurant in the small bedroom community of Ortonville, MI. There just wasn't enough population to validate success for the business. We partnered in the venture with Earl and Cathy VanCise; Earl was a fellow police officer, friend, and believer. My assignment was to be the general manager on a full-time basis, and they would work part-time according to their availability. Earl needed to remain on the department due to previous medical issues.

For several months, we struggled to find a way to make it profitable. We even hired a restaurant consultant. Harry was very knowledgeable and tutored me in the restaurant business to the tune of five thousand dollars. Many wrong decisions had been previously made, and after spending way too much of our capital, we discovered that we were unable to make a go of it. It was too late, and our ultimate downfall was revealed to be location, location, location!

Earl and Cathy wanted to try it on their own and decided to invest more of their life savings into it. Terri and I were financially unable to invest any further. We parted from our business relationship and gave them our blessings and prayers for success. Having no place to live since we had sold everything we had for the business, Earl and Cathy graciously offered us a place to stay up in their riverfront house in northern Gladwin, Michigan. A six-month rent-free agreement was granted to assist me in finding some new direction for my life and our financial future.

We accepted their offer, packed our personal belongings, placed everything else in storage, and headed north. It was mid-winter, and the whole family had to make sizeable adjustments. We also had a recently born son, Joey, who was a year old at the time. It was challenging for all six of us as our family moved to a remote northern area near Gladwin.

After living there for more than two years, we learned so much about lifestyle changes. We spent the first six months at Earl and Cathy's northern home as I sought local employment. I picked up some very low-paying restaurant consultant jobs to put some food on the table, but it was insufficient income for our family.

One of the most humbling things I ever faced in my life was seeking welfare support from the state. I did so and received food stamps to assist us with survival. We moved our family into a rental house on Secord Lake, and I begin to manage a small restaurant there. It was called "The Dam Restaurant" since it was right next to the Secord Dam. I renamed the restaurant "The Secord Family Restaurant" since I didn't like the double meaning of the word "dam." I treated it like a swear word, which was partially due to my narrow legalistic views and my declining sense of humor as a Christian.

Tossing my hat into the ring, I ran for sheriff in Gladwin County. The incumbent was Sheriff Larry Lawless. With a last name like Lawless, I thought I could beat him for sure. Running on the Republican ticket against him, I was easily defeated in the primary since being a newcomer to the county. The Democrat frontrunner was named McTavish. He frequented our restaurant and learned of my previous police experience. He subsequently asked me to run with him as his undersheriff. I agreed to do so and looked at it as a job opportunity with a potential income and became involved in the campaign process, but we still lost that election by seven hundred votes.

Our Gladwin years were very stressful, and we obviously struggled financially. Our oldest son, Jeff, went off to Barrington College in Rhode Island to pursue a marine biology degree, and we could provide little financial help. Michael, a senior, and Jennifer, a freshman, transitioned into Gladwin High School, and Joey was still a toddler.

Terri became pregnant with our fifth child, Carmelle. Carmie was born at Tolfree Hospital in West Branch. God took our low-to-no income, and thankfully we received complete financial assistance through Medicaid. Our entire hospital bill was provided through welfare, and we graciously thanked God. We simply had very little to live on during those years. We watched God be the provider—not Al Novak. God really did take care of us all the time, and we would often reflect on the many provisions that He provided continually for our family.

We joined a small independent Baptist church nearby. Secord Baptist was total countryish, but the people were loving, caring, and super kind to us. After some time, I began to teach an adult Bible study class. I always opened with a guitar solo entitled "He's Still Workin' on Me." And yes, God was still workin' on me in leaps and bounds.

Pastor Jaynes was the most loving and kindhearted person. He had little theological training and would prepare his Sunday message as we sang the morning hymns. Every three months, he would faithfully preach an old-time pulpit-pounding, evangelistic sermon. It was a typically fundamental and legalistic church, but they truly displayed love for one another. We fit in very well. Our little church had more than enough love to go around the room, and I needed to be around people who loved their families.

After a while, Pastor Jaynes asked me to serve alongside him in the pastoral ministry. Weeknight church family visits became routine. He would talk to the folks about everything—except spiritual things—like how the well pump was doing or gardening, farming, or auto and home repairs.

I would always ask, "When do we talk about spiritual things?"

He would say, "Brother Al, we just need to love people."

I found the love thing very hard to do after spending seventeen years in a police career that taught me to be cynical with people. God was re-teaching me, big-time, how to love others. After much prayer, I accepted the assistant pastor's position and was licensed by the church.

This was not a paid position, and we still had little income and very little sustenance. When our family sat down one evening for dinner, the five of us—Jeff was away at college—had literally nothing to eat except some peanut butter and white bread. That was it—and I am not exaggerating. I led in prayer as we prayed and gave thanks to God for the food. I thought to myself, *Is this really a proper meal to offer the family?* It was all we had, and it did provide us with something to eat.

Immediately after praying over our meal, we heard a knock on the door. It was a couple from our church family. Dale and Joanne Hodge were on our side porch, and they told us that God had told them to take some food over to the Novak family. They were holding two bags of groceries, which included a ham and an assortment of other foods. We thanked them; they did not know that God had used them to greatly minister to us and restore within us a renewal of our faith and trust in God as the provider (Jehovah Jireh).

There were so many miracles during that struggling time in our lives that Terri placed a list on the refrigerator for the kids to add events. It was called our "God Hunt" list. Each time we saw God show up and intervene in our lives, it would be added to the list. In no time, the list was full of God sightings in our lives. So, is God real? Oh, yes, He is!

After a year or so, Pastor Jaynes suffered a mild stroke. He was placed in the hospital and subsequently remained homebound for six months. My responsibilities were to take on the role as pastor and preach twice each Sunday and again on Wednesday evening for Bible study and prayer meeting. Visiting our church family members regularly included hospital visits when needed. God was growing me spiritually as I was introduced into this alternate route of learning to love others. This was one of the hardest things to overcome after my many years of policework.

When Pastor Jaynes returned to the pulpit, God had been really working in my heart about seeking full-time Christian service somewhere. I asked the church to pray with me. Please believe me that the whole church literally began to faithfully pray with me. God was listening to their prayers.

Several days after my prayer request was placed before the church, I was cleaning out an old file cabinet. On the bottom of a drawer, I saw a brochure about Forgotten Man Mission with a picture of Bill Most on the front. I had received this information several years prior from Pastor Bronkema. It said that Bill had been a Michigan State Trooper for eight years. The Kent County sheriff asked him to go to the jail and talk to the inmates about Christ. That was the beginning days of a statewide jail ministry that began in 1966, which became known as Forgotten Man Ministries (recent 2021 name changed to *Reach the Forgotten Jail Ministry*). FMM, having chaplains serving in thirty-five county jails in Michigan, shares Jesus Christ with inmates in a variety of evangelistic programs.

A Michigan mission program? Who would have thought it was possible? When I showed the brochure to Terri and pointed out that it was a mission program in Michigan, she thought that I should check it out. I wrote a nine-page letter, sharing my salvation journey as a police officer, and I mailed it to their headquarters in Grand Rapids. I ended the letter with the question: "Can you use a guy like me?"

CHAPTER 27

FMM Possibilities

The only thing known for certain at that time was that God would direct my path, and this was a firm belief. That is why my answer to God is always yes! Several weeks later, I received a phone call from Reverend Bill Most, the founder and director of Forgotten Man Ministries. A phone interview was conducted, and Terri and I were invited to drive down to visit their new headquarters on Fruit Ridge Avenue, which was just northwest of Grand Rapids.

Terri and I drove there and spent several hours on our visit. We were advised that there was soon to be an opening for the lead chaplain at the Genesee County Jail.

Bill asked me about my interest in the position and if I had ever been inside or seen the Genesee County Jail.

I told him no since most of my police work had been conducted in Oakland County. He said in his usual austere voice, "Well, before you even consider accepting this commission, I want you to contact Chaplain Mel Rykse, our present lead chaplain there, and plan a visit to see the Genesee County Jail firsthand."

Chaplain Rykse was transferring to the Muskegon County Jail

since he had family who lived on the west side of the state, and there was an opening at that jail. I contacted Chaplain Mel, and he invited me down to Flint. He suggested that I plan to stay with him—and his wife, Loie—and spend three days in the jail with him. I drove down to Flint, and we spent the next three days ministering in the jail.

Reverend Most suggested that Genesee County was the worst jail in the state of Michigan—and he was right! The jail had been under a federal consent judgment and was soon to be torn down. It was in a terrible physical condition and very unsanitary. There were cockroaches running everywhere, the pungent smell of urine and feces was noticeable in most parts of the jail, and the inside cell walls were plastered with pornography. Inmates often were transported to the medical unit to have cockroaches removed from their ears that had entered during sleep. The jail was filthy even though it was cleaned regularly. It was hard to share your faith and deal with many hate-filled attitudes from both the inmates and the deputies. That place was horrifying and felt like it was bathed in an evil presence.

Most of the deputies disliked having religious people on their floors. Chaplain Mel led me from floor to floor and from catwalk to catwalk. We would walk up and down the catwalks and talk to the inmates about Jesus. It was like being confined to the abyss of some underworld location.

Despite the many continual distractions and obstacles, we would clearly and audibly share God's Word and invite the inmates to receive Jesus Christ as their personal Savior. It always amazed me how often they responded and cried out to God with tears streaming down their faces as they asked God to save them. They would put their hands through the bars to pray with us and weep before God. People were being genuinely saved right before my very eyes. It was for real and not a show. For three days, as we prayed with those inmates, I was moved to tears in each housing unit. Jesus was their plea as God was saving them from their sins. As the song goes, "People need the Lord!"

One of the inmates on the sixth floor was greatly feared by the other inmates as being high up in organized crime (a.k.a. the mob). Greg was believed to be able to put a contract out on someone's life—and it was then completed by the underworld. Greg had accepted Jesus Christ as his personal Savior, and his whole life completely changed. He was determined to follow Jesus no matter what happened—even if it meant his life being taken by the mob.

Greg became the resident sixth-floor evangelist, and he excitedly grew in his faith as he voraciously studied the Bible. He subsequently led the whole 6-B block individually to the Lord. The deputies would often condescendingly request that we visit all the "Christians" up on 6-B. What a joy it was to share with the men there; they were so hungry to know more of God and His Word. There was entirely new life on 6-B, and even the deputies could see the difference. Evil had been forced out of the 6-B block and Jesus was now being proclaimed there.

Wow! Talk about being pumped up after three days! I was flying about as high spiritually as one could go. I knew I wanted to be in that jail because God was doing a phenomenal work there, and I wanted to watch God pour out His grace and grant gifts of faith to those sincerely seeking to be saved:

> "For by grace are ye saved, through faith; and that not of yourselves: it is the gift of God: not of works, lest any man boast." Ephesians 2:8–9 (KJV)

I drove back up to Gladwin, as my heart was bursting with the wonder of God's amazing grace in action. A few days later, Bill Most called to discuss my visit. He offered me the chaplain position and then asked me, "Al, can you live on seventeen thousand dollars a year? That is all we can offer you as a salary, and you will be required to go out and raise the total support that is needed in Genesee County."

Reverend Most did not know that our entire family had just lived on $7,600 income for the entire previous year. The immediate thought came to me, *This is a ten thousand-dollar pay raise. Of course, I can!* I said, "Yes!" However, if I had still been a police officer on the ROPD, I would have said, "No!" I was earning thirty-five thousand a year and working five part-time jobs, which brought my income to around fifty thousand a year, and we were living like we earned a hundred thousand a year—along with accumulating tons of credit card debt.

During those lean financial years living in Gladwin, God showed me that He would be our provider. It would not be the welfare system or the mediocre employment that I would occasionally find. It was God Himself. The challenges of raising the necessary support as a missionary at the Genesee County Jail needed to be fully entrusted to His provisional care. I had learned during our years living in Gladwin that He would supply our needs. I also knew that the jail ministry would only be sustained by and through Him.

On March 5, 1985 (seven days prior to the birth of our youngest daughter Carmie), my life entered a thirty-three-year honored position of watching God change the lives of so many people—from crime to Christ. My commitment to serve Him as the lead chaplain at the Genesee County Jail was now in place. New challenges to our faith began and we could not see the future ahead:

> "For we walk by faith, not by sight." 2 Corinthians 5:7 (KJV)

Before my final departure to Flint and being commissioned a jail chaplain with Forgotten Man Ministries, Pastor Jaynes wanted me to be ordained by the church. In a Baptist tradition of ordination, an individual must first declare that he has been called by God to serve in the Gospel ministry. This is usually done before his local church body. This church will then license him into the ministry after approval by a church vote. Other church leaders will consider his current role in the church and how he handles present responsibilities as evidence of a genuine desire to enter the ministry. When the candidate has accepted his first pastorate or commission, such as chaplain, the church will ordain him into the ministry, giving credence to his professed calling. Ordination is a one-time event for a Baptist pastor. It is not repeated if the approved candidate moves to other churches or ministries to serve. It is believed to be a lifetime calling conferred upon by God.

I asked Pastor Bronkema, my former pastor at Ortonville Baptist Church, to guide me through the preparations for the ordination process. Preparing a long thesis on my doctrinal beliefs and documenting them with scripture was the task ahead of me. A meeting was called to invite countywide pastors and church leaders to sit on a counsel and examine my written stated beliefs. Questions were asked, and it was up to me to defend my statements with scripture. This was done during a three-hour meeting, and the called-up counsel then approved my process of ordination.

In late February 1985, my ordination took place during a public ceremony at Secord Baptist Church in Gladwin. I was then sent out into the mission fields of Flint, Michigan (AKA Genesee County Jail). Following my ordination, I was officially "commissioned" by Forgotten Man Ministries to act as their authorized and approved jail chaplain. The title granted through a formal ordination is "Reverend." Following the Baptist tradition, the title of "Chaplain" was conveyed by the act of commissioning through Forgotten Man Ministries and recognized by the State of Michigan.

CHAPTER 28

Jail Beginnings

There was much to learn in the jail ministry. My initial training consisted of Chaplain Rykse handing me the ministry keys and bestowing a formal blessing: "May God bless you!"

The FMM chaplain's office was located on the third floor of the old jail. We had a very small room that was packed with stuff. The new ministry required a complete review along with re-organization and the need to devise a plan to increase our financial support. Everything was new, and a complete reliance upon God to show me the way was implemented.

My schedule in the jail began with four days a week, early morning until nearly midnight. Fred Brown, one of my volunteer associate chaplains, invited me to use an adjoining apartment at his duplex-home until I could relocate my family to Genesee County. So, on my three-day weekends, I would head back up to Gladwin to be with my family.

Being in the jail for four days in a row required lots of learning time, and there was so much to think about every day to coordinate this new ministry. My greatest joy was going out on the floors, sharing Christ with the inmates, and watching God at work. So many lives were being saved daily and it was such a blessing to see God move in miraculous ways.

The inside of the old jail was almost indescribable. It was very old and dilapidated and had been originally designed and constructed as a restrictive housing jail. Restrictive housing meant that most inmates were locked within individual cells in a row consisting of an eight-man cell block. The jail had been placed under a federal consent judgment to be closed or demolished. Under this judgment, Sheriff Joe Wilson was limited as to what he could enforce inside of the jail. Inmates were permitted to smoke in their cells, receive pornography in the mail, and use the vilest of language in the jail. The consent judgment prevented any changes until a new jail was built.

The jail was full of cockroaches, and they were basically unstoppable. They often entered the jail through the delivery of food boxes, and they would multiply quickly throughout the jail. Federal law permitted inmates to freely receive and plaster pornography all over the inside of their cells. These walls were often the backdrop as we stood in the catwalks and shared Jesus with them. This jail mirrored the muck and mire that permeates our world system and stands against our God and His Word. The world system is widely known as fame, fortune, power, and pleasure and promoted by the evil one

In addition, each of us acquired a sin nature at birth that keeps us apart from God. We were born with a dead spirit that needed to be born again and made spiritually alive in Christ. An inmate's life parallels the life that we all face as once stated in the scriptures:

> "Yet man is born unto trouble, as the sparks fly upward." Job 5:7 (KJV)

Have you ever poked a fire and watched sparks float into the air? God's illustration tells us that every person has lots of problems and man does not have to face them alone. The world system, the devil, and our own sin nature are all attempting to destroy us and keep us from knowing and loving God and having His partnership and help through our troubles.

When the chaplains would visit with the inmates, the deputies would have to open the catwalks and allow us to enter. They would then lock the door directly behind us with large, noisy, dangling jail keys. For that reason, the deputies were often referred to as "turnkeys" in the jail.

When I started as the chaplain in the old jail, there had been a few volunteer associate chaplains that were previously recruited, trained, and assigned over some of the varied ministries. They provided an assortment of outreaches to the inmates. For example, Associate Chaplains' Eddie Godwin and Louie Borsheim took book carts into the catwalks and distributed jail-approved items, including Bibles and assorted reading and writing materials.

Louie served the Lord in the jail ministry for more than forty years and was truly a godly man. Everyone that knew Louie was blessed since he was such a humble servant of the Lord. He would spend morning until evening in the jail every day, sharing with inmates, fasting, and praying, and overseeing the book carts. He was always available to help with any ministry endeavor and God used him to counsel and impact many lives. Louie is now at rest, awaiting the sound of the trumpet of God and the resurrection of the dead in Christ—a day we all look forward to with much anticipation. Thanks be to Jesus, our Savior!

Associate Chaplain Wilson Derr was another dear old servant who would roll a cart with a movie projector and show a Christian film inside the catwalks. The inmates would pull a sheet down from the top bunk and use it as a screen. An invitation would be given at the conclusion, and many would accept Christ. This media ministry was later developed into a video/tv cart process and faithfully continued for over 30 years by Associate Chaplain Charlie Ward. Charlie was saved after picking up and reading a gospel tract that Associate Chaplain Fred Brown had placed on an engine going down the assembly line at General Motors. Fred was an inspector and used gospel tracts often in his outside ministries. Fred invited Charlie into the jail ministry. Charlie also was a dedicated and sincere financial supporter of our jail ministry for all of those many years. Thanks be to God!

Many times, amid the smell of urine and feces in the cellblocks, we would share a Christ centered message from the Bible and give an invitation to receive Him as Savior. It always amazed me how often inmates would come up to the bars, kneel weeping, and reach their hands through to hold our hands as they repented of their sins, crying out to God and receiving Jesus Christ as their personal Savior.

Periodically during the daytime, inmates would be removed from their cells and allowed to walk to the end of the catwalk and enter a dayroom. Steel picnic tables were secured to the concrete floors, and the inmates would be permitted to lounge around the dayroom, move around a bit, talk among themselves, or even play cards, checkers, or other games. We would hand out the pre-approved games to inmates when resources were available.

Inmates were permitted to sign up for church services once a week. A preassigned church team would come to the jail with a few people and conduct a worship service. They came from a variety of local county churches.

Once a month, a ministry team came representing the Flint Council of Churches and would conduct a worship service. The preacher was Reverend Jonnie Kidd, pastor of a local Church of God in Christ. Jonnie, was our first Black associate chaplain. We also got to know and appreciate one another very well since we both attended classes together at the Flint Bible Institute. Jonnie was later honored and elevated to superintendent in his denomination.

Church services required a long time to coordinate and prepare each week. It was a slow process since only five inmates could be transported by one deputy at a time and escorted up to the sixth floor. An open recreation floor area had been temporarily converted into a jail service area. There was a piano, and many churches would have a piano player. Christian music in the jail always gave off an aroma of Christ. Miss Penny Roberts, who happened to be a full bloodied Apache Indian, was a daily volunteer with our team, and would make herself available in the absence of a pianist to play the hymns that were selected from the hymnbooks. Local churches would often provide us with used hymnbooks when they were purchasing new ones for their congregations.

As soon as the service was completed, an invitation to receive Christ was always given. After a short prayer, the inmates would be transported back to their cells, again moving five at a time. Some inmates would gladly attend the services just to get out of their cells for even an hour or so. God has His way of pointing people to His Son.

There were many noise distractions during our ministries that were conducted in the cellblock areas. Some inmates were not really interested in spiritual things, and they would sometimes cause disruptions to the services forcing everyone to be locked down. Satan has his way of creating division.

One of the most difficult areas in the jail to share Christ was in the lower intake level known as the bullpen area. Associate Chaplains' Walt Jones and Bill Stone would preach there twice a week. The bullpen was comprised of two larger holding units that housed four inmates per unit at a time. Because of the continuous jail overcrowding, eighteen or twenty inmates were generally waiting to be processed in each holding cell.

These inmates had been recently arrested and brought to the jail. They had to wait in the bullpen until an open bed could be found in the jail. The entire jail was designed to hold a total of 280 inmates, but it usually had more than five hundred booked in the daily count.

Walt and Bill would stand in front of those cells and speak as loudly as they were physically able, and they would preach from the Bible and proclaim Christ to those in the bullpen. Some inmates would angrily toss urine or feces on them, but that did not deter them from sharing Christ. Some of the others housed in the bullpen would angrily revile the defiant ones, and then just about all of them would come forward at the invitation to be saved. God was doing a great work there. However, the associates would often have to shower and thoroughly wash their clothes after arriving home to get rid of the putrid smells.

The reports from the bullpen ministry were always glowing. Those guys would always tell us how excited they were since many of the inmates who pretended to be asleep or looking away during their message were the first ones to line up in front of the bars and cry out to receive Jesus as their Savior. Thousands each year would come to Christ just in the intake area alone. We all were amazed about what God was doing throughout the jail, and so many troubled lives were being transformed from crime to Christ by simply proclaiming the Gospel of Christ.

Associate Chaplain Fred Brown was an Emmaus Bible College graduate, and he would oversee our Bible correspondence course ministry. He would distribute, collect, and grade the FMM Bible courses and then hand out award certificates to visiting inmates on a one-on-one basis to discuss their spiritual progress. Fred continued in this ministry for more than forty years in both the old and new jails. There were so many requests from inmates for personal visits to discuss spiritual matters that we were always overwhelmed and in need of additional biblical counseling volunteers.

My awareness of this need became apparent after a short time in the jail ministry. This was not a one-man show or even one that a handful of volunteers could satisfactorily provide. Prayer times were specifically set aside to ask God to send us more workers into these jail fields, which were truly yielding tremendous crops:

> "Pray ye therefore the Lord of the harvest, that he will send forth labourers into his harvest." Matthew 9:38 (KJV)

> "Say not ye, There are yet four months, and then cometh harvest? behold, I say unto you, Lift up your eyes, and look on the fields; for they are white already to harvest." John 4:35 (KJV)

There was a great need for committed Christian volunteers to assist us in meeting the spiritual needs of these inmates. Being invited to share about the jail ministry at many local churches became the platform that was used to invite those in attendance to pray for us, support the ministry financially, and if God was leading them in any way toward jail ministry, to seek us out and consider becoming a volunteer.

Each time—and in every church—an impassioned request would be made for prayer. Secondly, for volunteers to help us reach the forgotten inmates. Volunteers began to come one by one, and we later watched God increase our ranks to thirty-five associate chaplains and hundreds of other Christian volunteers who assisted in the day-to-day jail ministries. Every month, they provided many hours of personal biblical counseling to the inmates. I soon recognized that my job was to facilitate God's call on their life as they offered themselves to God for ministry service.

The female ministry continued to grow as we observed that more females were becoming involved in criminal activities and being housed in the jail. Our lead female associate chaplain was Sue Nolff, and she also was our administrative assistant. Sue continued with the jail ministry for more than thirty-five years and retired in 2021. She presently volunteers to teach a female bible study on Level 3. She was our only part-time paid staff member for all those years. Everyone loved Sue. She represented Christ in a very caring and loving manner, and she always made herself available to assist anyone with a need.

In the early days, Associate Chaplains' Barb Blough and Carolyn Bryers would minister to the females housed in the jail along with Sue and a few others. The female housing unit was always kept much cleaner than most of the other areas of the jail. My guess is that females are generally cleaner than males overall, but that's just an observed guess!

Starting in 1985, our yearly contributions began with only five thousand dollars of garnered support. The projected budget for my first year was thirty-two thousand dollars. Year after year, the budget continued to increase as new ministry programs were added. Our highest budget, after years of ministry endeavors, eventually topped out at $140,000 per year. I had no idea how to raise money or generate financial support. I also had no previous experience—none!

God however graciously reminded me of the time, while serving as a deacon at Ortonville Baptist Church, when we hired a new youth pastor. This fellow changed the whole dynamic of the church as he inaugurated the start of the youth ministry. Pastor Kevin Shorkey began with five kids in the youth group and built an exciting and vibrant ministry that eventually impacted the entire church. He did it very simply; he got people to pray.

He took five youth group participants out on a campout. He put baskets in the narthex by the door and placed the names of each young person attending the campout. He duplicated each name multiple times in the basket so that every adult had a name of one of the five to pray for. He requested that the church earnestly pray for just one person during that whole weekend. The church responded, and God really answered these combined prayers miraculously.

The youth group took off and became the focused spiritual excitement within the church. They began to grow and then doubled and tripled in size as the youth group grew to more than fifty kids who were really on fire for Jesus. The kids began to share their faith with their friends at school, and many new kids were saved and joined the youth group. The whole church had become spiritually revitalized through the power of prayer, and I witnessed it firsthand.

As the new jail chaplain, I was facing what seemed like insurmountable financial goals, and I recognized my lack of experience and confidence in these matters. I was dumbfounded. Just dealing with the everyday challenges in the jail, adding and coordinating new volunteers, and implementing new programs to share Christ with the inmates had filled my plate.

The added stress of raising needed financial support for the jail ministry placed a constant heavy burden on my shoulders. God had graciously reminded me through the example of Pastor Kevin that there was a way to get impossible things done: I needed to get people to pray.

Following his example, as invitations grew to share the jail ministry at our local churches, I would invariably beg people to pray. Specific prayer concerns were announced to the congregations, and prayer bookmarks were distributed as a reminder to pray for us.

The top priority of prayer was the much-needed financial support. Many of these committed Christians began to seriously pray, and God began to answer those requests, including the needed finances. These committed prayer warriors were also drawn from a variety of Christian denominations. God has a remnant of His people in every church, I observed.

As our budget grew each year over the next thirty-three years, we took in more than three million dollars of support in Genesee County. This averaged more than ninety-five thousand dollars per year in the third poorest county in Michigan per capita. Flint, Michigan itself is one of the poorest cities per capita in the entire United States.

Without further ado, let me introduce you to the One who did it! God alone is worthy of all the honor and glory forever and ever:

> "Yes, everything is for your sake, so that grace, as it extends to more and more people, may increase thanksgiving, to the glory of God." 2 Corinthians 4:15 (NRSV)

> "Whether therefore ye eat, or drink, or whatsoever ye do, do all to the glory of God." 1 Corinthians 10:31 (KJV)

CHAPTER 29

New Jail Transition

In 1988, a state-of-the-art jail was opened in Genesee County, and the old jail was later imploded using strategically placed dynamite charges that blew it into rubble. This new jail was designed as a direct-supervision facility and would house 384 inmates. The day we opened; we were housing more than five hundred inmates. Double bunking was subsequently added to each cell, and our daily population grew to more than six hundred. The sheriff, by court order, was often required to release inmates due to the maximum limits of the new jail.

The jail transition took more than a year. All the deputy staffing, including the jail chaplain, were bused out to Bucks County Prison, which was just outside of Philadelphia, Pennsylvania, to observe this type of facility in operation. There were only five "direct-supervision" facilities in the entire United States at that time. We went there to fact-find and interview personnel who worked in that facility.

Many of the deputies decided to quit since it was such a psychologically strenuous change from the restrictive housing format to having to deal with inmates on a personal basis. Everyone needed to learn interpersonal communication skills since frontline confrontation with inmates was the norm of direct supervision. This new system would require deputies to manage those incarcerated with no bars separating them, which was groundbreaking in jail management.

A unit generally consisted of fifty inmates and one deputy visually present in the area at all times. All parts of the housing unit could be kept under constant surveillance and directly supervised. There were no walls, doors, or bars between them in the open areas of the housing units. There were individual sleeping cells surrounding the open area that now were double bunked and contained two inmates each. Each floor deputy could electronically lock and unlock all the cell doors using the control panel. All other areas were open to the inmates.

Everything in the housing units were line of sight. Privileges of watching TV, inmate mingling, playing games, gathering at tables, using phones, participating in ministry programs, and many other perks maintained the actual control over the inmates—not the deputies. The concept of direct supervision was designed to save taxpayers money by reducing manpower within the jail. If an inmate violated any of the jail rules, they would be placed in a "restrictive housing unit" and lose all the privileges afforded to each inmate. Valuing these privileges resulted in general obedience to the guidelines since the inmates did not want to lose them.

Amazingly, after a few years of this transitioning process, the jail became quite manageable. The chaplaincy program had to be basically redesigned to meet the new facility security requirements, which necessitated many changes to our programs. Some former programs were discontinued, and many new ones were added over a long period of time.

One program at a time was started and guided through a trial period until it was proven acceptable before another new program was added. Our religious volunteers grew to visits of more than two hundred per month, and our Forgotten Man Ministries team of volunteer associate chaplains reached a high of thirty-five.

Becoming a religious volunteer in the jail required completing the Michigan Sheriff's Association Jail Chaplaincy Training Classes that were taught by Forgotten Man Ministries throughout the state of Michigan. The classes cost seventy-five dollars and included twenty-four hours of classroom instruction along with a syllabus and other reading materials. A criminal history check was completed on each volunteer, and there was a probationary period for all volunteers. All the rules and regulations of the jail were taught to each volunteer, and a complete guideline booklet with all the rules and regulations, policies and procedures, was handed out to each volunteer since they were required to observe all the rules. After one completed the classes, they would receive a sheriff's ID pass and be permitted to visit an inmate, teach a Bible study class, or assist the jail chaplain.

If someone was interested in becoming an associate chaplain, after completing the chaplaincy training classes, they would work as a volunteer with the FMM team for at least a year before filling out the paperwork and being interviewed for the position. Once approved by the home office in Grand Rapids, they would be commissioned as a volunteer associate chaplain and receive credentials for that appointment. They would minister directly under the supervision of the lead chaplain appointed by Forgotten Man Ministries.

Our ministry budget rose to $140,000 per year and was very challenging. During those struggling years, Flint went from having thirty-five thousand good-paying General Motors jobs reduced to five thousand in a city of more than one hundred thousand people. The income level had drastically diminished in our county, yet God miraculously sustained and expanded the jail ministry throughout those years. Did we always meet our budget? No. Our county budget often was subsidized by neighboring counties that were overfunded. Why did God not fully fund this work? We prayed and prayed to that very end and stay tuned for the answer. It may surprise you.

Beginning with a few associate chaplains in the old jail, we witnessed God increase our ministry team each year. Christian volunteers continued to join God in His work at the jail as so many lives were being touched and changed by His amazing grace. The gospel of freedom was being proclaimed and declared to those behind bars. Jesus is our only answer and He is our arbitrator before God pleading our cases individually. (1 Timothy 2:5). Thanks be to God.

CHAPTER 30
Chaplaincy Classes

One of the highlights of being a part of the jail ministry was sitting back and enjoying the jail chaplaincy training classes that were taught each year in the Flint area. Reverend John Fehler, the FMM executive director and successor for Rev. Bill Most, completely re-developed the entire course and became the chief instructor. John was also appointed the designated chaplain to the Michigan Sheriff's Association. FMM and MSA combined and offered regional jail chaplaincy training classes to religious volunteers at different locations throughout Michigan during the year.

John would pack all his materials, books, handouts, and media equipment and drive across the state to offer jail chaplaincy training for volunteers who were interested in knowing how to minister in a jail setting. The course consisted of twenty-four hours of classroom instruction. It was open to anyone that was interested in jail chaplaincy and began with a four-hour session on a Friday evening and then eight hours on Saturday for two weekends.

Locations and facilities were provided by each county host chaplain. Genesee County served as the host of four or five surrounding counties as a regional training location. Some classes were conducted in churches, halls, available rooms, and college campuses. Attendance varied from fifteen to more than a hundred. After completing the training classes, one would begin as a basic religious volunteer in the jail under the supervision of the county jail chaplain. Some would set their sights on becoming an associate chaplain with FMM, but this took time and required additional instruction and participation in all the different ministry programs that were offered to inmates through FMM.

The goal was to properly prepare Christian volunteers to enter their local county jail and minister safely under the guidance and permission of their elected sheriff. This training included learning the security concerns of the sheriff and the available ministry opportunities in the jail. Each county jail was different and had individually designed and varied housing confinements.

Jail ministry is different and generally has many more obstacles to deal with than other Christian ministries. There are many distractions and interruptions in the jail all the time, and security measures constantly beleaguer those ministering in the jail.

One could be teaching a Bible class or sharing in a one-on-one biblical counseling session with an inmate, and a jail alarm may go off to warn of a disturbance, a fight, a medical problem, or a weather emergency. They had to stop whatever they were doing since all the inmates were immediately locked down, and the volunteers had to go to a designated safe area and wait for an authorized return. These situations happened very often in the jail, and the procedures needed to be learned and followed without hesitation.

John's training assisted volunteers in preparing for these in-house jail situations. Occasionally, a deputy might project a negative attitude toward the religious volunteer. The training taught the volunteer how to respond and handle the situation with kindness.

Each chaplaincy volunteer was advised to permeate the aroma of Christ in the jail and follow in His footsteps. One certain jail adversary was the devil, and his troops, that would always stand against you:

> "For we are the aroma of Christ to God among those who are being saved and among those who are perishing; to the one a fragrance from death to death, to the other a fragrance from life to life." 2 Corinthians 2:15–16 (NRSV)

Jail ministry was certainly not the service road for everyone, as it took time to learn the guidelines and prepare for the many ruts and potholes to be faced along the way.

John made the classes great fun even though there was much to read and learn. Part of the class was to read a large book, *The Christian Counselor's Manual*, by Dr. Jay Adams. This was included in the curriculum along with studying the syllabus on jail chaplaincy, and it contained lots of valuable instruction and information. John would take most of the highlights of the syllabus and discuss them in the classes. He included fishing tips, humorous jokes, and personal stories from his life. The best part of the training was the abundance of laughter in the classes. Laughter played a vital part in the class and would break up the tedious sharing of all the ministry information that had to be reviewed. John could take a wearisome, long curriculum and present it with such humor that those hearing simply had a good time, unless one was a stick in the mud.

I attended more than thirty years of class sessions taught by John and never found them dull or boring. John was a great teacher and would encourage classroom discussions. The final exam was given on the last day of class with a hundred-question test. One needed to pass the test to get a completion certificate; if they didn't pass, the local chaplain would assist the volunteer until they understood the materials, completed the class, and were issued the proper credentials.

Sheriff Joe Wilson and Sheriff Bob Pickell—whom I served under during my thirty-three years as the chaplain—required that all religious volunteers attend and complete the training classes to reduce the sheriff's liability in the jail. It also rooted out those who may have questionable motives for going into the jail.

Each year, I looked forward to coordinating and attending the classes taught by Reverend Fehler, and I always learned something new. There was so much to learn about jail ministry. Those years were spiritually beneficial to the thousands who attended the classes—even if they did not follow through with future jail ministry plans. They would also learn some great fishing tips since John was very close to being a professional in the art of catching fish. I think he could have written a best-selling book on fishing!

I am so grateful to God for allowing me to enjoy such times under John's instruction and for serving under his leadership over Forgotten Man Ministries for so many years. I never had a person complain that they did not like the training classes. Laughter is good medicine, and John made this proverb very relevant.

John and I also found some time to hang out together outside of the ministry. John was an ex-Marine, and he loved to find adventures in the great outdoors when hunting and fishing. I also enjoyed adventures, but I really wasn't looking for them. We sometimes hunted white-tailed deer together in northern Michigan.

One year, we found a place to hunt on state land in northern lower Michigan. We split up and headed in opposite directions to a predetermined hunting location. I found my spot looking down a long open power line trail at the edge of some woods. As I sat there, a large doe entered the runway. It was a long rifle shot, but I had a scope on my rifle and a doe permit license. Personally, venison wasn't my favorite choice of meat, but John liked it—and we could always give it away to folks who would be happy to have it.

Carefully taking aim I looked at that deer through the crosshairs of my scope. Instantly I had a memory flashback to my rookie police days and the barricaded gunman declaring that he had me in the crosshairs of his scope. A sudden chill went down my spine as I thought about his clear-cut view of me at that time and God's shielding me of certain injury or death.

I fired one shot but failed to calculate the trajectory of the bullet at that distance. Since the shot was more than two hundred yards long, I only wounded the deer. Tracking it way back into a swamp led me to hundreds of deer tracks going in every direction. The blood trail had finally stopped, and my disappointment and sadness set in.

On my way back to meet John, I was walking in an open field and inadvertently stepped into a larger puddle that was unknowingly composed of Michigan quicksand. My body quickly sank down to my shoulders, and it continued to suck me down into this slough of despair. Acting quickly, I stretched out my arms and found a resting place to horizontally land my rifle to slow my body's descent.

By God's grace, I was able to keep pulling, tugging, and lifting my body out of the sucking sand. My hunting clothes were totally covered with liquid muck, but I was able to make my way back to our meeting spot.

I excitedly told John about my harrowing encounter with the quicksand and my near-death experience.

He shouted, "Yeah, life is an adventure!" John loved adventures.

I wasn't so enthusiastic about the whole ordeal, and it still lives in my memory bank as a very close call with death. I thought, *Yeah, life is an adventure, all right!*

During those ministry years, God was also teaching me to be content with my wages. This was an extremely hard thing for me to learn. The early years of my employment with Forgotten Man Ministries was under the leadership of Bill Most. My beginning salary was seventeen thousand per year. Despite all the miracles God had performed in our family, assuring us of His provisions, my own sinful nature of harboring discontent swept through my spirit.

Bill Most resigned as the mission director, and John was appointed by the FMM board of directors to fill his position. John sacrificially and remarkably led Forgotten Man Ministries for thirty-four years and grew the ministry teams from eleven chaplains to thirty-five chaplains serving in our Michigan county jails. Prior to John's leadership, the mission had several years where the chaplains pay was withheld for months due to a lack of funding. John pledged that the chaplains would never again have to deal with payless paydays under his leadership, and he kept his word for all those years.

My fundraising efforts continued to increase—and so did my constant requests from John for pay increases. Each year, salary bumps were sought. Whether I deserved it or not, my pay never seemed to suffice and meet our family's expenses. Our needs grew as we helped our kids through high school and college and all the additional expenses connected with child rearing. I became aware that our heavenly Father had tolerated enough of my constant discontentment.

Reading in the scriptures shortly after I had requested another pay increase from John, God spoke directly to my heart through Jesus' own words:

> Likewise the soldiers asked him, saying, "And what shall we do?" So he said to them, "Do not intimidate anyone or accuse falsely, and be content with your wages." Luke 3:14 (NKJV)

> Let your conduct be without covetousness; be content with such things as you have. For He Himself has said, "I will never leave you nor forsake you." So we may boldly say: "The Lord is my helper; I will not fear. What can man do to me?" Hebrews 13:5–6 (NKJV)

God clearly pointed out to me that my dependence was to be completely upon Him alone and that He was Jehovah Jireh (the Provider) for all my needs. Reflecting on all the circumstances in my life since my new birth and recognizing God as the absolute provider during our Gladwin years, it became very clear to me that I needed to wait upon God and learn to be content. My continual dissatisfaction with my wages was to cease and it was time to surrender my full trust in Him alone for all our family needs. I did not need to ask for pay raises any longer, and it was time to change and follow God's Word. My decision was to ask our heavenly Father when I needed something and to only ask Him.

I met with John once more to apologize for my discontent over my salary, and I asked his forgiveness for my constant requests for pay increases. I let him know that there would never be another such request. God had spoken to my heart that I needed to be content with His provisions and that he would take care of all my needs. I never again asked for another pay increase over the many years that I remained as an FMM chaplain. God wanted to show me that He was "Jehovah Jireh" and positively confirm in my heart that He is the best Provider!

To God be all praise, honor, and glory. Amen!

CHAPTER 31

The Wisdom of Marilyn

One of the wisest and most supportive women I have come to know during my thirty-three years as the Genesee County Jail chaplain was Marilyn (Vander Woude) Terpstra. Marilyn was hired by the Forgotten Man Ministries back in the 1960s when she was only nineteen years old.

FMM was started by Bill Most, a former Michigan State Police Trooper and an eight-year veteran officer. Bill was asked by the Kent County Sheriff to go into the Kent County Jail and minister to the inmates. Bill was a devout Baptist believer whom God had called upon in 1966 to inaugurate the formation of Forgotten Man Mission, which later became Forgotten Man Ministries and presently known as Reach the Forgotten Jail Ministries. Marilyn's father, George Vander Woude, served as a Forgotten Man chaplain at Kent County Jail for forty-four years and served humbly as the custodian at the home office on Fruit Ridge Avenue and in 2007 began his rest in peace.

Marilyn began as a secretary and served Forgotten Man Ministries more than fifty years, advancing in her leadership positions with FMM. Our paths crossed during my chaplaincy years with FMM. Each county jail chaplain had their own unique set of difficulties and often battled discouragement with support-raising efforts or managing internal jail problems.

Marilyn supervised the entire home office and served in a leadership role to Ellen and Donna, our part-time office employees. She would also oversee all the volunteers who assisted with daily ministries at the home office. These included correcting Bible courses and packing, sorting, and mailing out promotional materials.

Most importantly, Marilyn became the chaplains' frontline advisor and preliminary counselor to our growing number of lead jail chaplains who were ministering in these Michigan county jails. She was often the chaplains' first line of communication when troubles occurred. There were many times that just being down in the dumps would necessitate a call to Marilyn.

Amazingly, God gave Marilyn a special gift of ministry as a helpmeet to each chaplain. She had a supernatural ability to untangle and decipher problems and suggest ways that often completely resolved the issues at hand. She was always able to point me in the right direction and lift my spirits if they were down. How does someone know exactly the right spiritual uplifting words to say, apart from God, unless they are His chosen instrument?

There were times when I was going to quit over some troubling issue, and she would be able to completely understand exactly how I felt and talk me through it over the phone, enabling my heart to find rest and resolve. This gift could only come from God.

Marilyn was so much more than an advisor and counselor. Over the years, we developed a deeper friendship that included much laughter and many heart-to-heart conversations—usually through phone calls or emails—that brightened both our days. Marilyn was a person who God put in one's life to impart His perspective, which is wisdom, on the matter at hand and assist one through those pending problems and troubles.

Thank you Father for Marilyn and her ministry in my life during the thirty-three years serving with FMM, in Jesus' Name, Amen.

She retired in 2020 after more than fifty years of serving our wonderful Lord and Savior Jesus Christ. She was a special friend to many chaplains and volunteers, and we pray God's blessings upon her retirement years.

Lightheartedly joking with her one time, I explained that she will be sitting in the front row when we gather in the heavenlies someday. I said, "If you hear a voice shouting way in the back, 'Marilyn, Marilyn,' please put in a good word for me with the Lord!" It would be me hollering up to her from the back row. She laughed.

Each one of us believers will be in that room only because of God's grace and the shed blood of Jesus Christ, our Savior, covering our sin. Since we all are equal at the foot of the cross, may I say, "Thank you, Marilyn, for a job well done for the Lord—and may all praise and glory be given to our God —knowing for certain that this would be her response."

CHAPTER 32
Moving into Grace

In my earlier years as a jail chaplain, I determined that some systematic theology was needed to assist me in jail ministry since I did not have any formal seminary training. Even though I had spent many hours personally studying the Bible for years after my conversion, I had not put it all together completely. Previous recordings on cassette tape of Pastor J. Vernon McGee's "Back to the Bible" daily broadcasts and then later recording all of Chuck Swindoll's radio messages would be listened to repeatedly in my squad car. Replaying them continually throughout my tour of duty became a daily source of biblical instruction. A cassette tape player was connected to the cigarette lighter for power and enabled me to listen as often as possible throughout my policework day's activities.

Most often riding in a one-man unit enabled me to listen throughout the day to these teachings when I was not responding to a dispatch. There was a year or two that the department put us on ten-hour shifts, and I was growing every day in my faith and learning more about God's Word.

After several years of listening to Chuck Swindoll's daily

radio broadcasts, he began teaching a series called "The Grace Awakening." Having become a full-blown legalist already, this teaching struck a deep chord in my heart. It was like pouring cool water on the hot flames that had entrapped me. My attitude toward other Christians began to turn around. My eyes of understanding were opened to God's amazing grace and how it saves people and keeps them also.

An awareness of looking down with contempt on other believers emerged and I recognized this attitude as wrong in my spirit. The "Grace Awakening" teachings brought me a breath of fresh spiritual air that poured into my soul. Uncovering this reconfirmed grace relationship with God pointed me back toward seeking intimacy with Him. God also used Chuck Swindoll's short book, *Intimacy with the Almighty*, to point me in the right direction. It became one of several spiritual resources that God used to change my direction.

Randy's suggestion of reading the Bible word for word began my spiritual training along with his discipleship. It continued through the preaching and teaching of the Word by sound Bible teachers and pastors. My spiritual growth was significant in those years, but it did not enable me to tie all the spiritual truths together systematically.

Realizing a need to lay out my theological beliefs from A to Z, the time had come to get some formal footing into my faith. One of our faithful supporters during those early years of jail ministry was Sunshine Bible Shop in Flint. Their store was located only a few blocks away from the jail. Mr. and Mrs. Farber, the owners, were generous and caring Christians who sacrificially helped missionaries and other believers. They would generously give whatever they had to assist those in need demonstrating their deep love for God through their works. They were strong supporters of the jail ministry and the Novak family as well.

Flint Bible Institute, abbreviated FBI, was founded by two graduates of Dallas Theological Seminary, Don O'Dell and Leo Reynolds. It was a bible training institute that focused on God's Word and His grace. It was situated in the rear section of Sunshine Bible Shop, through the generosity of the Farbers' and it thrived on a very tight budget with limited resources. The Farber's additionally provided a tuition-free scholarship for FMM associates to grow in their faith. The only thing needed was for the student to pay for their books. Many of the classes offered only required a Bible as the textbook.

For ten years of part-time classroom instruction, I pursued this systematic theological training to get my beliefs methodically organized and thoroughly understood. Some classes were offered during the daytime, and some were evening classes. They covered a wide spectrum of preparation studies like Dallas Theological Seminary. I was able to complete most of the three-year seminary degree, but I lacked the Hebrew classes and a few other subjects.

Earlier I had discovered the Grace Awakening that opened my eyes and pointed me to a way out of legalism. The radio broadcasts and books of Chuck Swindoll were the stepping-stones that God used to draw me out of it and moved me forward into a grace perspective. FBI confirmed all these beliefs through years of scriptural study and Biblical resolutions.

Flint Bible Institute was a place of profound grace teaching. An example of such instruction was demonstrated in one of my Greek classes. At the beginning of my Greek exegesis class, Leo Reynolds, our instructor, said, "Today, I am placing an A in your grade for the entire class."

I thought he was kidding, but that is exactly what he did. He told us that we didn't even need to open a book or study any Greek at all since we had already received an A for the entire class. The A was already documented in his record book.

I was astonished as this illustration itself was an amazing teaching tool. He said, "That is exactly what God has done for us personally." God has granted us an A in salvation. He granted us this A—by grace—that mirrored exactly how God saves us through faith. It is a gift from God, and there is no effort needed on our part. No class studies are required:

> "For by grace you have been saved through faith, and this is not your own doing; it is the gift of God— not the result of works, so that no one may boast." Ephesians 2:8–9 (NRSV)

Eternal life is knowing the one true God intimately (John 17:3). Yes, we were freely given a "salvation A" with no strings attached. God placed this A in my grades, which I certainly did not deserve and did not work for it as most students are required to do. God pours out His love upon us by grace and looks only for our return of love back to Him.

That grade illustration enabled me to understand God's amazing grace and how He offers this same grace to everyone without exception. His grace fully captivates us into loving Him with all our hearts, souls, minds, and strength. Do you recall how Jesus answered the scribe in Mark 12 when he was asked this question? "Which is the first commandment of all?"

> Jesus answered, "The first is, 'Hear, O Israel: the Lord our God, the Lord is one; you shall love the Lord your God with all your heart, and with all your soul, and with all your mind, and with all your strength." Mark 12:29–30 (NRSV)

No one deserves God's favor since we are all sinners. He forgives us with no strings attached when we put all our faith and trust in

His Son Jesus as our Savior. All our sins are replaced with an A. If you have received that A in your salvation journey, rejoice with me, dear reader! Jesus paid it all.

Bit by bit, stepping away from legalism and moving into grace had become my greatest crossover since it led me back to chasing intimacy with God. God began showing Himself to me as I had never understood before.

Another adventure that God opened to us was to build a new house. It required a full commitment to the day-to-day construction process and required me to drop my FBI classes just short of receiving my diploma. This project encompassed land development which led to house construction and ultimately became a ten-year project. It required eight years of my blood, sweat, and tears as I worked on the house as often as possible. By God's grace, the house was completed, and we were blessed to move into our new earthly home that was situated outside the city in a rural area. There are so many God stories that could be shared throughout the entire construction process, but it would most likely require another book. However, I will share here a few God stories to bless you.

We had been living in a nice city neighborhood, Mott Park area, in Flint for about ten years. Joey and Carmie, our youngest of five children, grew up there on Thomas Street. The kids had a neighborhood *Flint Journal* newspaper route, and it had become home for us. We had many fond memories of living there for a total of seventeen years.

However, the area was changing. Several drug houses moved into the neighborhood, and an illegal auto repair garage moved in across the street from us. The neighborhood began to change for the worse with noise and drugs.

One morning at the breakfast table, I said, "Terri, maybe we should build a new house somewhere outside of Flint." I had acquired previous building experience on two houses in Ortonville.

She looked at me and said, "How can you build a house when you do not have any property?"

Her question kind of set me back on my heels, and I brusquely responded, "God will provide us the property!" I really did not think that God would give us some property, but I said it in rebuttal.

I began my search for a lot in the nearby community of Flushing. They were overpriced and not affordable for us, but I did like the general living area. At one of our twice-weekly prayer meetings at the jail, I mentioned to my prayer team that I was looking for a lot to build a new house. I asked them to pray with me for God's direction.

Three days later, during a visit with a businessman who supported our jail ministry, I presented the idea to him.

He said, "Why do you want to build in Flushing?"

I said that I had no reason other than I liked the area and the small-town atmosphere. He said that he had lived there for some time, but he later moved into Genesee Township. He said he purchased land, and his kids all went to Kearsley schools. He liked that area very much.

He told me that he still owned a ten-acre parcel, which had been detached from his house, which he eventually sold. His kids had used the land for snowmobiling and horseback riding. He said that he was tired of paying the taxes on it and had no use for it anymore. He said that if I wanted it, I could have it. I nearly fell out of my seat as God had undoubtedly provided the property! I was totally astounded with this gift of land.

He later quit-claimed the property to me and told me that the parcel was landlocked, but he would get a right of way from the power company to put a road into the property. He did exactly that. I couldn't wait to tell Terri that God had provided property for us to build our house. The property was gifted over to us, and we had to plan a way financially to construct a house. I spent many hours clearing the land, praying, and asking God to show me the way.

The property consisted of ten square acres. We were granted a right of way into the property by Consumer's land management, and for eight years, I struggled through the process of developing the land. My initial idea was to divide it into four parcels, sell three of them, and use the proceeds to build our house. After speaking at a church in Grand Blanc, a man named Budd came up to talk with me. He was one of the owners of Davison Land Surveying. I must have mentioned my desire to develop this property and build a house during my message, and he told me that he would like to help us out.

He told us that he would provide all the surveying services upfront and wait for his payment until we sold off some of the land. Our designs went from four lots to fifteen lots, to twenty-nine lots, and the final revision was set on twenty-seven lots. Taking a builder's licensing class and having previous construction knowledge enabled me to acquire my Michigan Builder's License.

Spending weeks reviewing a three-foot stack of house plans did not reveal the exact house design that I was looking for. After purchasing a home designer computer program, I was able to completely design our house, room by room. My plans were detailed enough that when we finally began construction, the rough-in carpenters were able to build entirely off these plans, which saved me from having to provide blueprints.

Prior to the construction stages of our new house, it took eight years to develop the property and get the required paperwork completed, which generally would take two years for a professional land developer. We purchased another 2.6-acre parcel and added it to the land, enabling us to negate using the power company's access road. We redesigned the plans to include a two-thousand-foot private road into the property. This was the final revision.

The last stage was set to start the project and construct the road. It was time to wait upon God to provide the bulldozer and the means of completion. We prayed.

Budd called me up during that waiting period and told me that he had a land developer in his office who was looking for some land to purchase. He did not want to go through the normal two years of tedious paperwork, which had taken me eight years to complete. This man purchased the land from us and gave us some cash to cover our accrued expenses. We also kept four choice lots out of the twenty-nine as our buy-out package and thus began plans of our future house construction on one of the lots.

This man then invested $650,000 and put in a county-spec paved road, underground utilities, and sewers, and had the property professionally land shaped. It was a spectacular transformation, and after all these changes we were finally ready to build our house.

We procured a construction loan and completed the basic house in two years. There were many God sightings during those two years, which enabled us to move into our new house in 2006. After moving in and within five years I was able to finish off three bedrooms in the basement and two more in the bonus room upstairs along with several baths to accommodate our entire family get-togethers, which had grown to twenty-four persons. Our children and grandchildren live in four different states, including, Michigan, Ohio, Virginia, and Arkansas. We love our family times together even if it is only twice yearly. I generally fry up ten pounds of bacon, and it is gone within two days. We have lots of laughs and much fun together as a family—all because of God's amazing grace and His abundant provisions. I also had not asked for any pay increases from FMM and learned that:

> "... godliness with contentment is great gain."
> 1 Timothy 6:6 (NKJV)

Thanks be to God for the ten years of study at Flint Bible Institute that enabled me to clarify my biblical understanding of God's grace. Systematically I was able to formulate a theological position and sufficiently enabled to stand on my beliefs. This also made me realize that I would always remain a student of the Word. A student is forever open to learning and must not succumb to the sin of dogmatism (know-it-all-ism).

During one of my classes at Flint Bible Institute, a special awareness of God's grace became so prolific. We were studying through the book of Galatians, and I was instructed to circle every word that referenced grace. During that class, so many questions were answered concerning the depth of God's love for us and how He continually pours out His grace upon us. God constantly does this to enable us to discern His individualized love for us so that we might pursue intimacy with Him. It is His grace alone that demonstrates His love for us, forgives us all our sins, and grants us eternal life to come:

Grace, grace, marvelous grace!

CHAPTER 33

Our First Housing Miracle

In 1986, we moved our family from Gladwin to Flint. Starting as a new chaplain at the jail required a search for adequate housing for our family and ultimately a move to Flint. Three different times after locating a house that would meet our needs, the same results would surface after applying for a mortgage. The response was always, "Mr. Novak, you have insufficient income to meet the mortgage payments—denied." They were correct, but this was my salary and all we had to live on. Yes, seventeen thousand dollars a year was insufficient income to meet our family's housing needs, but a journey down contentment road was in progress.

God was soon to perform another miracle to reconfirm that He had really called me into the jail ministry. Being very disappointed about not being able to afford a house for our family, I soon realized that there was nothing else to do but pray.

I asked some of my associates to pray with me about finding a place in Flint for our family to live. Associate Chaplain Carolyn Bryers attended West Suburban Bible Church. She spoke up after our prayer time and mentioned that her church had two parsonages that were provided for their lead and youth pastor. She said that both were unoccupied at that time as the two pastors had been called to different ministries. She asked me, "If either house were made available as an option for us, would I be interested?" My reply was positive, of course.

Carolyn spoke with one of the elders who called me back that very next day. The church had supported Forgotten Man Ministries for several years, and they were very interested in helping us out. A meeting with the elders was scheduled, and they gave me a tour through both houses and asked which parsonage I would be interested in using if the church approved.

The lead pastor's house was extremely nice. It was located a mile away, but the youth pastor's house was right next to the church. I told them that either house was great, and that my only concern was getting our family back living together again. They told me that the proposal for allowing us to use one of the houses had to be posted in the church bulletin for two weeks before a vote could be taken.

It was a Friday, and they had to quickly reprint a new church bulletin and include the notice for the upcoming and following Sundays, which they did. Ten days later, they called me at the jail and said the church had voted to allow us to use the youth pastor's house. We could move in as soon as we were able. Ten days after we prayed to God, He provided us with a miracle house to live in.

I asked the church elders what my expenses and responsibilities would be for the house, and a short list was given to me. The only things we were responsible for were paying the utility bills and keeping the house reasonably clean inside and outside since folks coming to church would pass by in the parking lot during scheduled meetings. If we couldn't meet the utility bills, they even offered to assist us as well.

They gave us keys to the church so we could use the gym attached to the church along with any of the church facilities, if needed, like the church kitchen and hall if we would like to have our family gatherings on Thanksgiving or other occasions. We were invited to use the baseball field in the back when not in use, and hiking trails led to some beautiful woods. It was a phenomenal place to live, and the house was more than adequate in size and comfort.

The following weekend, we moved our family into the parsonage. By the time we packed everything up into a U-Haul and drove several hours to Flint, we were totally exhausted. It was a very cold night as we arrived in the moving van at two thirty in the morning. We informed them that we would be arriving sometime that day. Three of the elders—Roy, Bill, and Jerry—waited all day—no cell phones then—and all evening to help us carry in our belongings. God had one blessing after another for us as we got to know and fellowship with these warmhearted, loving believers.

After settling in, we subsequently joined as members of the church. Our family attended all the services with much joy, and the church continued looking for a lead pastor. I was able to assist with some pulpit supply and lead some Bible studies.

One of our most concerning financial difficulties was that even though the FMM chaplains had a salary, they were at times unable to pay the chaplains their designated salaries. This was due to a shortage of generated support during seasonal times of the year. During one such shortage period, the payless paydays lasted for thirteen weeks before I received any pay at all. Again, I was learning where to turn in time of need and requested prayer support from my ministry team at the jail. We bathed these concerns in prayer and waited upon the Lord.

God answered my concerns in an amazing way after each Sunday morning service for the next thirteen weeks. Mr. and

Mrs. Farber were also members of West Suburban Bible Church and attended all the services. They would always stop and ask me how the ministry was going. Mrs. Farber (Margaret) would also ask me if we had received our pay for that week. Each of those thirteen weeks, I would lower my head humbly and respond with a no. She would motion to her husband, Wayne, whisper something to him, and point toward us. He would walk up to me and place two hundred dollars of cash into my hand. Week after week, for each of those thirteen weeks, God continued to supply our daily needs and show us that He was Jehovah Jireh. The Lord desires sometimes to demonstrate His care through miracle provisions. He used Mr. and Mrs. Farber's availability as His instruments to be our sustainer during these dry times. I have often compared these provisions with the manna (found in Book of Numbers, Chapter 11) that God faithfully provided for the Israelites as they wandered in the wilderness for forty years. He provided their needed sustenance each day. God likewise was faithful to us each day providing us with bread to eat. Jesus did say that he was the bread of life (John 6:48).

In addition to these blessings, our daughter Jenni had been facing a difficult transition during her junior year of high school moving from Gladwin into a completely new public school system. She hated the public school that was nearby, and she felt so alone and became very discouraged. She did not like her new teachers and could not find any friendly students in her classes. There were lots of cliques within the student body.

Mrs. Farber somehow heard about our concerns for Jenni. She took a grandmotherly interest in her and developed a special relationship with her. In addition to their ongoing support of our ministry, she offered to provide the tuition for Jennifer to attend Genesee Christian High School. What a difference this made in Jenni's life. She absolutely loved Genesee Christian along with her teachers and soon established some lifelong student friendships.

God supplied all our personal needs during those difficult years and completely confirmed in my heart that He really had called me into the jail ministry. There was so much more for me to learn in the days ahead about trusting in the Lord.

We lived in the parsonage for three years, and we were able to establish an employment record with Forgotten Man Ministries. As time went on, we became eligible to purchase a house in the Mott Park area. That was an area of Flint that had once been occupied by General Motors medium-income executives. Since GM had downsized so drastically, the area had become available and was convenient to the jail. We really were blessed as a family to live there seventeen years. During this time, four of our children had married and moved to different states and our youngest graduated college.

God continued to show us miracles with His provisions both for our family and in the jail ministry. Living life as a faith missionary and waiting upon God was teaching me every day to walk by this faith.

CHAPTER 34

Experiencing God

We were members of South Baptist Church from 1989 until 2003 and living in Mott Park. I began to develop the parcel of land that we had received from Virgil, served also as a deacon at the church, and ministered daily at the county jail. Time became very precious since all these endeavors required a portion of it.

Joey and Carmie, our youngest two children, were involved in the youth programs and participated in many of the other church programs at South. They loved being a part of our church drama teams and youth ministries, and Joey learned to play the guitar for youth group functions. We were in "happy land." We had many friends, Bible study groups, and enjoyed personal spiritual growth. Our Bible study group decided to embark on a six-month study through a syllabus workbook. Henry Blackaby's *Experiencing God* was selected as a daily journal and guide through this study.

Our Bible study group had spiritually connected in an intimate way, and we began to really practice brotherly love for one another. Each of us began to experience God in unique ways. Blackaby's book was all about "knowing" God and doing His will. I spent many extra hours bunny-trailing through this journal, and I would look up every reference verse that was given and spend time seriously contemplating relevant applications to my life. It was like having a guide through God's Word pointing out one personal application after another.

Dan, our group leader, was able to draw us all out of our shells that resulted in meaningful participation during our discussion periods. We began to recognize one another as naked sinners bound together in God's love. We were venturing through the portals of experiencing God.

What does "experiencing God" really mean? It means knowing about God and finding a personal connection with Him; after all, He is a real person. We were created in His image, right? Some of the things I learned during this study were:

- God is always at work around us.
- God is pursuing a continual love relationship with us that is genuine and personal.
- God invites us to participate in His work.
- God speaks to us though His Word, prayer, circumstances, and other believers to reveal Himself, His purposes, and His ways.
- God's invitation to join Him requires the yielding of oneself, and it will bring us to a crisis of belief that requires faith and action.
- Major adjustments in our lives may be required when joining with God.
- One comes to know God by surrendering all to Him, obeying Him, and allowing Him to accomplish His work through us.

This study was so helpful to me, and it was a stepping-stone to a yet undisclosed deeper journey alone with God. It pointed me in the direction of chasing intimacy with Him as there was more to grasp. Eternal life is finding intimacy with our Heavenly Father:

> "And this is eternal life, that they may know you, the only true God..." John 17:3a (NRSV)

> "He went up the mountain by himself to pray." Matthew 14:23b (NRSV)

CHAPTER 35

Miracle Dog

Carmelle, our youngest daughter, wanted a dog. She was in the seventh grade and was deeply involved with the youth group at church. She had often and repeatedly asked me for a dog over the past few years. We have a generationally separated family: first a family of five, and fifteen years later, a family of four. The first three children—Jeff, Mike, and Jenni—grew up in Ortonville during my police career days. Joey and Carmie grew up in Flint during my jail chaplaincy years. The older Ortonville kids had all kinds of pet animals. We had several dogs and cats, ducks, a hamster, a rabbit, an iguana, and a bird—and all the challenges and trials that go along with raising them and then losing them to death. My days with pets were decidedly over. My mind had been set and determined not to have another pet in our house.

Carmie, our sweet late-born daughter, wanted her own pet dog. At first, I just said no. Her requests continued in different ways and times. My answer remained the same: no. There was always a sympathetic explanation given to her of how sad it was that she missed growing up with the older kids who had all the pets. I was sad for her, but we were not going to have any more pets in the Novak household. That did not stop Carmie. She turned to her youth group and asked them to pray that we would get a dog. Her dad was learning to do the same thing at the jail, get the group praying.

Often at church, walking down the hallway, one of the kids from the youth group would come up to me and say, "Mr. Novak, we are praying that Carmie will get a dog!"

I would say, "Well, quit praying because Carmie is not going to get a dog. Sorry!"

Dan, our adult Bible study leader, heard of Carmie's request. He handed me two hundred dollars and told me to use the money to buy doggy essentials like a water dish, shots, cage, and whatever else was needed. I tried to hand it back to him, but he walked away.

I said to him, "Dan, we were not going to get a dog."

He said, "Well, use it wherever."

I just shook my head and kept on walking.

My thinking led me to try a bit of common-sense psychology. Maybe Carmie needed to see the whole picture. I compiled a "Bow-Wow contract." I printed out, in a large font, fifty things that Carmie would have to be responsible for if we got a dog and a place after each requirement for her to initial if she accepted that requirement. Examples: 1. Purchase the dog license____ 2. Feed the dog every day ____ 3. Take the dog out when it needs to go ____ 4. Get the dog his shots ____ 5. Clean up if the dog makes a mess ____. The list totaled fifty responsibilities that would be required of her as a dog owner.

My goal was to make her completely aware of all the dog responsibilities and duties that would be required of her and that her eyes would be opened to these tasks. My hope was that she would change her mind and scratch the whole idea of wanting a dog.

Well, to my disbelief, Carmie returned the Bow-Wow contract—fully signed and initialed in each location. My idea had failed to change her mind. We remained steadfast in our disagreement. I told Carmie that I was sorry, but even though she had completely signed the contract, we were still not going to get a dog—and that was final.

She was very sad, but my feet were firmly planted. I thought to myself, *In a few years, she would be going off to college, and Terri and I would ultimately end up assuming all the dog care and responsibilities. No way!*

Each FMM county chaplain was required to attend a bimonthly daylong chaplain's meeting in Grand Rapids. The meetings provided us with updates, opportunities for chaplain fellowship, new ministry information, and strategies to assist us in fundraising. For years, I had been serving as a county jail chaplain and as the Eastern Michigan District chaplain. In addition, on occasion, I was asked to serve in the capacity of an assistant director.

In March 1999, I drove to our scheduled meeting in Grand Rapids. Sadly, it was just after rejecting Carmie's signing of the Bow-Wow contract. While driving to Grand Rapids, it was my custom to audibly pray to God. Recapping the whole story to God of Carmie's desire to have a dog and my reluctance over the responsibilities of dog ownership, I shared with God my sadness over Carmie being heartbroken because of my denial. Praying for Carmie and the entire situation concluded with a final petition (like the fleece of wool – found in Judges 6:37) to God: "However, if you put a dog at my feet, I will take it home to Carmie." My immediate assumption was that this would or could never happen. After my challenge was laid out before God, my prayer time concluded as I arrived at our home office. By the way, it is not a good idea to challenge God and expect your own conclusion.

I was twenty minutes early for the meeting. When I entered the doorway of the home office, three or four puppies were scampering around the main aisle.

I asked Marilyn what was going on.

She said that Chaplain Terry had brought in some recently born puppies in hopes that one of our chaplains might want one. A day earlier one of the pups had been grabbed by a barn owl, and he was looking for a safe home for the rest of the litter.

While I was speaking to Marilyn, one of the puppies came running up to me and laid down placing its little head on my shoe and fell asleep.

She said, "Do you want that puppy?"

I immediately responded, "No, but I am probably going to have to take it home!"

She had no idea of the reason for my response, and she certainly did not know of my challenge to God within the last hour. I tried to gently move the puppy's head off my foot. I was totally dumbfounded that this cute little ball of fur was content to remain sound asleep at my feet. My prayer request had been answered—quickly, amazingly, and miraculously.

God gladly took up my challenge and showed me that nothing is impossible for Him. He also honored Carmie's childlike faith and her heart-to-heart prayer requests and those of her youth group. God made it clear to me that I was certainly obligated to take the puppy home. That is also the reason one should never challenge God; it could backfire on you.

Marilyn was a bit puzzled. She did not know that it certainly was not my will—but His alone:

> "...nevertheless not My will, but Yours, be done."
> Luke 22:42b (NKJV)

When the meeting ended that day, I put the puppy in a box and drove back to Flint. I was really very excited to see Carmie's reaction when she received her dog. The whole situation was a faith builder for all of us, and Carmie was so excited that God had answered her prayers and kindly took on my little challenge that amazingly increased my faith and made me wiser.

We raised "Aussie" from a puppy and had her for almost twelve years as a family pet. Using the two hundred dollars that Dan had given us for doggy items became a real blessing. Aussie, however, was an obstinate dog and needed much training. Carmie did take care of the dog most of the time until she went off to college, and we continued to care for her through those years as predicted.

In 2007, after Carmie graduated from college, she took Aussie with her to live in Plymouth, Michigan, and then to Ohio, and she had her for another four years before Aussie died. My conclusion in all of this is that God can do impossible things and yet He is always on your side. Avoid challenges to God since it could sidetrack your life. There is so much power in the sincere, faith-filled prayers of a young child, and quite frankly, aren't all of us who truly believe in Jesus God's children?

> But Jesus said, "Let the little children come to me, and do not stop them; for it is to such as these that the kingdom of heaven belongs." Matthew 19:14 (NRSV)

CHAPTER 36

Performance Theology

We sat under several pastors during our years at South Baptist Church. One former pastor had theologically moved from legalism into grace, and his preaching became extremely refreshing and encouraging. Our Christian lives took on a new excitement experiencing a release from the bondage of legalism. Most of the church was being set free from these shackles. Trouble soon began to brew from the legalists who appealed to the overseeing council of the General Association of Regular Baptists. Tremendous pressure was applied on our pastor from this group and those legalist members of the church that he finally resigned. Several years later, he left the pastorate completely and pursued a law degree becoming an attorney. He simply had enough pressure and contention that many of us grace advocates completely understood. Legalism is a brutal adversary, and it will leave a foul spiritual taste in your mouth.

The new pastor preached a Christ-centered grace message

about once every six weeks. When preached, my comments would always be encouraging to him: "Pastor, that was a great message today!" Then there would be five weeks of saying nothing to him. The five in-between weeks I termed as "performance theology" messages. These types of messages are consistently and normally preached in conservative churches. Certainly, if you have been a practicing Christian in a conservative church for any period, you have heard many of these sermons. Let me explain the difference.

A performance theology message is one that takes the Word of God and pinpoints a work that needs to be done. The question is inferred, "Why haven't you done this for God?" As the Word is exegeted, it is always used to challenge the believer to act. It is a pep rally call to perform for Him. Therefore, I call it "performance theology".

My dear reader friend, if you are a believer, God wants you to simply make yourself available to Him since He really needs you on His team. He wants to perform through you. Yes, God needs you, but He alone must receive all the honor and glory. Performance theology tends to create a process of good works that often robs God from His rightful glory because we believe that we are doing the work. Our prayer should be like this: "Dear Heavenly Father, I do not want to ever perform for you, but please know that I am available to You today. Lord, feel free to use me in any way that You choose with no strings attached. I am aware that it is Your desire that everyone needs to hear about Jesus. Amen." A popular Christian song that immediately comes to mind is "People Need the Lord."

During my seventeen years as a police officer, our first three older children would say, "Daddy, do you have to go to work today?"

"Yes, kids," I would say. "Daddy has to go to work!"

After transitioning into the jail ministry, our younger two, Joey and Carmie would ask the same question, "Daddy do you have to go to work today?"

I would say, "No, Daddy doesn't work! He just goes to the jail and watches God do all the work."

The only question God ever asks us is, "Are you available for me today?"

Performance theology is going to work for God, yet God is simply asking us to be available to Him so that He can work through us. God has lifted the weight of performance from our shoulders. His burden is light and simply necessitates an offering of oneself. This results in a spiritual fulfillment simply knowing that you were used by the true and living God. What an honor and a privilege it is to worship Him this way! Amen.

> "And so, dear brothers and sisters, I plead with you to give your bodies to God because of all he has done for you. Let them be a living and holy sacrifice—the kind he will find acceptable. This is truly the way to worship him." Romans 12:1 (NLT)

My prayer each day as I entered the jail was always the same: "Lord, feel free to use me. I am available today!" I realized it wasn't up to me to change lives, but God could use me in that process if I was available to Him. We rob God of His rightful glory when we perform for Him and take the credit for the results. This is the danger of performance theology.

Jail ministry volunteers would often say, "I got ____ people saved today!"

"You did? My, aren't you wonderful?" Is the picture getting clearer? Are you seeing my point? This is what I mean by performance theology. Who gets the praise and glory?

My journey with God started with an intimate connection. Learning and practicing formal religion established good moral conduct during my youth and then being born again into the spiritual realm generated a natural tendency to draw me back toward religion.

However, religion is a covering used by humans to look good in the sight of God. The very birth of religion is when Adam and Eve sinned and disobeyed God, and then they became aware that they were naked and covered their bodies. That covering (a.k.a. religion) was and is insufficient. God had to properly clothe them before they were removed from the garden. He needed to provide the correct covering (clothes) for them to wear and this required the shedding of blood:

> "And the Lord God made garments of skins for the man and for his wife, and clothed them." Genesis 3:21 (NRSV)

A garment made of skins meant that some animal had to die. Jesus died and shed His blood to cover all our sins. His blood became our cleansing before God, and it provided complete forgiveness for every sin we have committed and will ever commit:

> "But if we walk in the light as he himself is in the light, we have fellowship with one another, and the blood of Jesus his Son cleanses us from all sin." 1 John 1:7 (NRSV)

God continued to open my spiritual eyes, which enabled me to understand that His plan of salvation was by grace alone through faith—and not of works at all (Ephesians 2:8–9). Performance theology is basically a system of self-imposed works (working for God) as opposed to God working through you. Grace and doing something for God (works), according to the scriptures, do not align themselves together. Performance theology is not included in God's grace plan and shows itself as another false covering of religion.

So, dear Christian reader, please know that when you avail yourself to performance theology, you are basically robbing God of His rightful place of worship and withholding some or all of the honor and glory that only belongs to Him.

May your prayer go something like this: Thank you, Father, for freeing me from my own good works and using me to worship You with my sacrifice of praise. I am available to you today, please use me in the name of your Son to bring You all honor and glory. Amen.

> "Through Him, therefore, let us at all times offer up to God a sacrifice of praise, which is the fruit of lips that thankfully acknowledge and confess and glorify His name." Hebrews 13:15 (AMP)

CHAPTER 37

Jail Ministry Grows

The jail ministry grew during those early years, and our frontline associate chaplains were the ambassadors of Jesus for all the programs offered daily to the inmates through FMM. My part in God's program was to facilitate His call upon their lives. Each person had a special ministry gift that God had given to them, and I needed to recognize their heartbeat and appoint them where they could be best used to bring glory and honor to Him.

Preaching teams were formed, and special areas were assigned to evangelize inmates. A Bible course department was set up in the jail. Fourteen "Back to the Bible" study courses were handed out to inmates, and they could register to take the entire sequence of studies. In addition, advanced courses were offered through our home office. All the copyrights were subsequently purchased by FMM, and the Bible courses were later published under the Forgotten Man Ministries label.

After an inmate would satisfactorily complete a course, an award certificate was handed to them. Amazingly, for many it was the first positive reinforcement in life that they had ever received—just a simple award certificate with their name on it. Inmates would often share this Bible study award with their families, which gave their loved ones some hope for a positive change in their lives.

The old jail was scheduled to be demolished and imploded using dynamite charges. Three years had passed, and God continued to do a great work there. Many inmates came to Christ in the muck and mire of this aging, filthy, and deteriorated facility.

In 1987, after my second year at the old jail, I recognized my need for a secretary to assist me with paperwork and general office duties. After sharing this need one Sunday while speaking at Ambassador Baptist Church, God spoke to that perfect helper's heart. Sue Nolff completed the twenty-four hours of jail ministry training classes and became eligible to join our team. She was later hired as a part-time secretary or office assistant and was to oversee the female ministry in the jail.

Sue was assigned a side office and conducted the day-to-day administrative duties that included scheduling all our group Bible studies and church worship services and coordinating all our fundraising dinners and events. In addition, she biblically counseled many female inmates who requested her visits.

Sue continued to serve the Lord at the old jail, and when we transitioned to the new jail, she remained faithful to God's call for thirty-five years. Sue also trained up an ever-growing number of female associate chaplains who ministered daily to the female inmates. People do need the Lord, as the song goes, and both male and female people were being saved daily in the jail.

Getting a Bible into the hands of a requesting inmate was an important daily ministry. Our home office purchased soft covered Bibles for distribution in all our county jails. We could order what we needed for our individual jails and pick them up at our monthly meetings along with our Bible correspondence courses. These were equated onto each chaplain's budget resulting in the need for additional financial support.

We followed this procedure for many years until we were invited to a meeting with our local Genesee County Gideon camps. They offered to supply, without any charge, all our soft cover Bibles and pocket New Testaments to hand out to inmates. It was such a blessing, and it saved more than five thousand dollars per year from my escalating budget. The Gideons are an amazing group of believers who love the Word of God and are truly worthy of financial support for their ministry endeavors.

Transitioning into a new "direct supervision" jail required many changes. A book cart program for the inmates was re-organized in the new jail. It supplied spiritual and wholesome reading materials on a weekly basis. Several of our supporting Christian churches set up collection locations for used Christian books and magazines to help supply our book carts. This program became very successful, and we also handed out Gospel tracts, *Our Daily Breads*, pencils, writing paper, envelopes, and an assortment of security-approved items to the inmates during our weekly visits. Each item that an inmate received came with the words, "God loves you!"

Each Christmas season, we sent out an appeal letter for donations to purchase approved inmate gift items. The FMM team would pack the gifts into hand-decorated Christmas bags by kids from local churches and pass them out to the inmates. This was normally done as close to Christmas Eve as possible. Gift items included an orange, apple, banana, a Christmas Gospel tract, a pocket calendar, some additional spiritual literature, a Christmas pencil, a candy cane, and some good-quality chocolate candy. The fresh fruit had to be excluded later since some inmates were caught making hootch out of the oranges and apples. The ingenuity of some of these men always amazed us! Of course, the majority suffered the loss of the fresh fruit during this special season of giving. We of course would share the gospel and give a salvation invitation to the inmates prior to receiving their Christmas gift from God who loves them very much.

Another plan that was tried and failed was our cassette tape ministry program. One of our associate chaplains and generous supporters, Barb graciously funded the complete cassette tape program. We purchased cassette players, thousands of blank cassettes, a high-speed cassette tape duplicator, and Christian music, and we copied hundreds of Christian messages and music tapes. Barb and Virgil were faithful and generous supporters of the jail ministry for many years.

Shortly after the initial transitioning into the new jail, the inmates had an electric outlet in each cell that was GFS circuit controlled. The ground fault was set for five amps, and the breaker would trip and shut the complete circuit down to prevent any inmate from getting hurt. The new jail permitted the sheriff to ban smoking, and we became a smoke-free facility. Many of those inmates addicted to cigarette smoke had transitioned over to the new jail and reacted very badly to quitting cold turkey. I fully understood this from my previous personal addiction and battling through the struggles of nicotine withdrawal.

Inmates would get their loved ones to conceal and bring in cigarettes on personal visits. The problem surfaced with lighting the cigarettes. Creatively inmates devised an amazing way to light their cigarettes without matches. Carefully stripping and removing the graphite from two of our book cart pencils, they would place the lead pieces carefully into each side of the electrical outlet without touching one another.

Dampening a piece of toilet paper, they would lay it across the two graphite pieces creating a circuit and the paper would ignite quickly to light their cigarettes. Most often, it worked very well. The smell of cigarette smoke could be easily detected through the air duct system inside the jail.

One of the problems with this system was if the toilet paper was too wet, it would not ignite the paper—but it would cause the breakers to pop and shut down the entire circuit. This required our maintenance personnel to constantly reset the breakers, which was very time-consuming, and they began to complain.

Simultaneously, our cassette tape ministry program supplied new believers with Christian Bible teachings and music that they played on small, corded cassette tape players. This ministry was very encouraging and enabled inmates to gain significant spiritual growth. Since the electrical circuits were constantly being tripped by the smokers, those inmates with players were not able to listen when the circuits were down. The maintenance department were also resetting the circuits at a much slower pace.

The handwriting was on the wall, and they finally shut down the circuits permanently—and no one could use them. This action was devastating to our Christian tape ministry program, and we had to completely strategize a new way to continue it. Many inmates reported to us of significant spiritual growth as they listened to the ministry tapes.

After thorough examination, we cut all the cords from the cassette players and decided to use rechargeable batteries. We bought four rechargeable D-size batteries for each unit along with a new supply of charging stations. By God's grace, all these items were donated. We began by distributing one cassette player to a qualifying inmate for one week at a time. Each week, we would replace the batteries with freshly charged ones. This worked for quite a while. Sadly, to report that a few of the inmates had taken the batteries out of the units, placed them in socks, and used them as defense weapons against other inmates. This of course required that ministry to be shut down for security reasons. We pooled our ideas and tried to figure a way around the problem.

One of our associate chaplains, Don Talbot, was also a

mechanical engineer. He meticulously thought through the situation. He sought advice from his colleagues and challenged them to find a way to design a battery locking system on the cassette players. After several months, they came up with a new defensive design. Torx-head hardened-steel screws were placed in a locking frame that fit entirely around the unit and fully prevented access into the battery compartment.

We purchased electric screwdrivers with torx bits to open and close the units and quickly replace the rechargeable batteries. The program was reinstated and lasted unabated from any security issues for several more years. The cassette tape ministry was very successful, and many inmates were really growing stronger in their new faith in Christ.

Satan wasn't done of course with his continual attacks, and we all know that he comes to steal, kill, and destroy. An inmate arrived in the jail from state prison for a court case. He was very ingenious, and I think he was inspired by the devil himself. There are some very talented people in our prison system, and Satan enjoys toying with them. His purpose always has been to keep people from following Christ.

This prisoner somehow was able to remove the frame and completely disassemble the entire cassette player. He detached some vital internal parts from it and designed a tattoo machine out of it. He was later caught tattooing other inmates using the dismantled cassette tape player parts. That was the straw that broke the camel's back. The security of the jail had been breached sufficiently to force us to discontinue the cassette tape program. We were sad to end this ministry and a decision needed to be made regarding disposal of all the cassette ministry materials.

Subsequently, we donated all the players, thousands of cassette tapes, batteries, battery-charging systems, and frames to the Flint Carriage Town Ministries. This Christian ministry reaches out to the downtrodden, poor, needy, and homeless people in the community. It was a great blessing for them since they endeavor to share Christ with our street people, many of whom are former jail inmates.

The cassette tape ministry was a spiritual blessing for those inmates who sincerely desired to grow in their new faith, but it proved to be non-workable in the jail. Satan does win some battles, but in the end the Bible declares, he will be defeated completely and cast into the lake of fire. PTL!

The most statistically impacting jail ministry programs that we were able to start was called the GRO Pod (God Restoring Offenders). This was an eight-week volunteer biblical training course for inmates. It included six hours a day of biblical instruction in daily Christian life skill applications. A variety of topics were taught from the Bible that included marriage intervention, anger resolution, prayer life, and intimacy with God. The curriculum included video media from selected Christian instructors and Bible teachers.

Associate Chaplain John Heyworth was our initial GRO Pod instructor, and we used a course of study that utilized basic life principles. Associate Chaplain Dr. Thomas Saunders, author of *Choices*, donated his books and designed a visual curriculum protocol. He taught it weekly for eight sessions. Associate Chaplain Jerry Cesal instructed "anger resolution" classes, and Associate Chaplain Leo Wynne later led the entire group daily. Other teachers were added along the way, and all student questions were welcomed as a tool of instruction. Many hours were spent in topical discussion intervals as part of the curriculum. Classes consisted of twenty-five to thirty-five volunteer students who would rotate in and out according to their availability as they were moved through their due process of law proceedings of their court cases. Some inmates spent over a year in the GRO Pod.

Hundreds of students over the years were able to complete the entire GRO Pod training classes and would consistently testify as to having a genuine change in their lives. Through this discipleship program they learned to love God with all their hearts and obey His Word. Many would request to audit the course again—if space permitted—to learn more about God. The program statistically verified an impressive reduction in the overall recidivism or rate of return to jail. According to statistics, two out of three inmates (76%) would return to jail in the first three years after release. Those students that completed the GRO Pod program, only two out of ten (21%) returned to jail after eight years of keeping records. This meant that more than half did not return to jail. Each inmate that did not return to jail saved the taxpayers an average of twenty-six thousand dollars a year—or more—in just housing costs. The former inmate also greatly benefited with a new life in Christ and became a better parent and neighbor. This was a win-win situation for everyone.

God is in the "by grace through faith" cleaning-up business, and the lives of these jail inmates are certainly on the heart of God. After all, He sent His Son, Jesus, to connect us to Him in an intimate, personal relationship, resulting in a promised eternal life to come.

By the way, Jesus hung out with this type of crowd during His life here on earth, you know the sinners (with a sizzle tone on the word sinners). He offered them and us freedom from the punishment for our sins and a new life simply by putting our faith and trust in Him. The offer is hard to refuse and pass up since all things in one's life becomes new again. What a tremendous offer to start over with a whole new life!

> "Therefore, if anyone is in Christ, he is a new creation: old things have passed away; behold, all things have become new." 2 Corinthians 5:17 (NKJV)

CHAPTER 38

Prayer Team

The most fruitful ministry endeavor at the jail was our prayer team. Starting in the old jail, an invitation was given to our associate chaplains to meet with me on Fridays to pray. After our prayer time ended, Associates' Walt Jones and Bill Stone would go down into the bullpen area and preach to the inmates. This area was considered by many to be the pit of the old jail. It was a large open area cell with one fully viewed toilet on the back wall, and it was intended for maybe four inmates to be housed at a time; however, it was often packed out with eighteen to twenty-five inmates. This was a holding area for those who were waiting to get booked into the jail. Some of them would spend a day or two waiting for an open bed in the main jail.

Walt and Bill would constantly report amazing responses to the Gospel being preached in that area. Inmates would appear to be sleeping during their preaching time, but when an invitation was given, many of them would immediately get up, come to the bars, and cry out to be saved. A prayer of salvation was offered for them to share in, and almost everyone would pray out loud and ask

Jesus to save them. How many of them were really saved? Only God knows the answer since salvation is found only in Jesus.

> "And there is salvation in no one else; for there is no other name under heaven that has been given among mankind by which we must be saved." Acts 4:12 (NASB)

We recognized that God was working in our very presence, and we considered the results directly related to our prayer times. Walt suggested that we meet and pray on Wednesdays and Fridays since we observed so many of God's incredible answers to our prayers. Thus, it became our practice twice weekly to pray throughout the remaining years of our jail ministry. God was not only hearing our requests but answering our prayers in a phenomenal way. I am certain that for the Christian, prayer is the best way to get anything done.

Going back to 1986, our prayer team began crying out to God for His guidance, help, safety, wisdom, and the salvation of the inmates. We asked God to use our ministry programs to bring people to Christ. We prayed that God would meet and supply the needs of the jail ministry through increased financial support. As a faith ministry, we completely depended upon God's provisional supply. Our prayer times were not social functions and we sincerely got down on the knees of our hearts and implored God for His help. The prayer team continued to grow, and after we transitioned to the new jail, we would normally have eight to ten associates meeting twice weekly for prayer. May I comment that this is the power of God in action that gets things done His way. I believe that every Christian ministry needs a committed prayer team.

As speaking invitations would come to share the jail ministry at our local churches, these became wonderful opportunities to share what God was doing in the jail. Christians along the way were volunteering and committing to pray for us. Most of the volunteers that God had called into the jail ministry came from those times of sharing. Often, I would set up and use a large multimedia slide presentation to share the jail ministry with the church.

One Sunday morning in the early days of our jail ministry, an invitation came to share the ministry at Colonial Hills Baptist Church in Montrose. Terri and I packed up our old beat-up Ford Escort and loaded my table display and the bulky multimedia dual slide projector unit. We also had to find space for Joey and Carmie. Joey was sitting in the back seat underneath some equipment, and Terri was holding Carmie in her lap on the passenger seat.

Arriving at the church, it was like a re-enactment from the Beverly Hillbillies TV series. With our loud muffler and beat up old car along with one door rattling loose from its hinges, we pulled up to the church chugging our way to the front door. We arrived early to set up the multi-media equipment, ministry displays, and the handout materials prior to the morning worship service.

Terri said to me as we pulled up to the church, "God is not providing our needs!"

I was amazed at her comment and responded back concerningly, "He is. We made it, didn't we?"

She expounded saying that the car was just barely running and had more than two hundred thousand miles on it. Carmie was just a toddler, and she rode all the way there without any restraining device. With all the equipment on board, there was no room left for a car seat. Joey was barricaded in the back seat under all the equipment. She said that it was not safe—and that God was not providing our needs.

Thinking of her comments, we began to unload the car and set up the displays. Terri was a very godly woman, and when she spoke to me about anything spiritual, it was generally to my benefit. She was my loving wife and ministry partner—and God gave her great wisdom in matters like that.

After the service, we drove home. I began to contemplate further Terri's analysis about God's lack of provision. Our salary was seventeen thousand dollars a year, which wasn't that much, but I believed that our needs were being met.

We were living in a church parsonage at West Suburban Bible Church and only had to pay for our utilities. This provision of God was given to us after our ministry team had prayed. With Terri's observations in mind, I began to focus on getting a better vehicle. I asked our prayer team at the jail to pray with me for God to provide us with a minivan. I figured that a vehicle like that would enable our family to travel safely together and carry all the needed FMM equipment for future ministry presentations.

After a Sunday morning service, a couple from the church told us that they had been saving money for quite some time and that God had directed them to give it to us as a gift. On the way out the door, Gary handed me a check for $5,000. He told us to use it for a down payment on a car or for whatever we needed. We sat in the parking lot stunned, shaking inside with joy, and kept praising and thanking God.

On the following Friday, the prayer team began to ask God to provide a minivan for us. I had been previously looking in the paper for a used Dodge Caravan since it would be the right size to meet our needs. They were a hot buy at that time, and as soon as one was listed in the classified ads, it would be sold. There were none offered in the paper on Friday when we first prayed together.

Another issue was to figure out how to pay for a car. After a detailed analysis of our financial picture, the highest monthly payment that our family budget could afford was $108 per month.

On Sunday, I scanned the classifieds and noticed an ad for a 1986 Dodge Caravan with fifty-four thousand miles on it. The owner said, after calling her on the phone, that she had a buyer from Canada who wanted it—and the price was a firm $7,600. The buyer was to come and get it on Monday, and it appeared that we had missed this opportunity. At the conclusion of the call, I left her my phone number if there were any changes.

On Monday morning, the owner called us back and said that the buyer from Canada was caught in a snowstorm and was unable to come and see the van. If I was still interested in it, I could go over to see it. We jumped in the car and drove there during a heavy snowstorm with more than ten inches of fresh snow on the ground. The minivan was in Clio, Michigan, about twenty miles away.

The owner showed us the Caravan, and I asked her for a test drive. She said that she would go with me to answer any questions. The van was exactly what we needed and very clean with low mileage. After arriving back at her house, I said, "Would you take seven thousand dollars for the van?"

She sat quietly for a few moments and said, "Do you realize that I had the van appraised, and that the lowest wholesale price on it was $7,600."

I told her that I realized that it was worth every penny she was asking, and it certainly was wholesale priced. My research had previously revealed the market pricing on Dodge Caravans, and her price was beyond fair.

I asked her again, "Would you take seven thousand dollars for it?"

She looked at me and told me with a bewildered look on her face that she would.

By God's grace, with the $5,000 gift previously received, we were able to procure a car loan and purchase the van. We drove that van for another two hundred thousand miles, and it met our every need, including a seat belt for each of the kids and a place to store all the ministry equipment in the back. Our monthly car payment came out to be (you guessed it) exactly $108 per month which was the maximum amount that we could afford.

God continued to provide all our needs. Prayer is the tool to use when seeking God's help. Yes, Pastor Kevin from Ortonville Baptist, you were right; all it takes is to get people seriously praying! This story doesn't end there by any means but continued as there were many more vans on the way by God's grace through prayer.

Forgotten Man Ministries continued to grow with newly appointed chaplains being added to our county jails in Michigan. Our director, Reverend John Fehler, asked me to take on the added role of Eastern District Chaplain. This included additional responsibilities to assist our chaplains on the eastern half of Michigan when they requested it. Guiding new chaplains in setting up their jail ministries was also part of this role. This often included attending fundraising dinners, delivering supplies, and serving as an advisor to our newer chaplains. Some would call me with questions about troublesome issues in their jails or seek ideas about starting new programs in their jail. FMM continued moving forward by God's grace.

The most important item on my agenda was to encourage participation and attend our Wednesday and Friday prayer meetings. I was thoroughly convinced that prayer is how to get things done and with each answer God confirmed my conclusion. These were days of building faith, trusting in the Lord, and watching God provide solutions to our petitions—even including miracles of healing.

Praying even for some antagonistic floor deputy resulted in amazing outcomes. After a while, the deputies who were formerly against us would be calling the chaplain's office to request a visit for a troubled inmate. Many deputies enjoyed our visits on their floors and our personal time spent with them. Prayer was changing everything inside and outside of the jail and it provided complete optimism and encouragement over those many years.

God faithfully continued to bless and provide vehicles for me to drive. Whenever we had a need, the first place to go was to God in prayer. During our regular weekly prayer meetings, I asked our associates to pray with me about supplying another vehicle since my Dodge Caravan had reached its end. The associates poured out their hearts to God and asked Him to give Chaplain Al a new van. I wasn't asking for a new van—but simply another vehicle—and a good used reliable one would be all I needed.

Three days later, I received a phone call from one of our generous business supporters. Virgil was a local businessman who was a believer and very supportive of our jail ministry. He had a prodigal son who had been in jail several times for misuse of prescription medications. His wife, Barb, became one of our female associate chaplains and supported the work as well.

Virgil said, "Hey, Al. Go over to Jim Waldron's GMC/Pontiac dealership in Davison. They have some customized vans on the lot. Talk with a salesman named Travis and take one for a test drive!" Then he abruptly hung up. That was all he said.

I had absolutely no other information of what was emerging. I called Travis, and he informed me that Virgil had asked him to show me some vans on the lot. After driving to Davison, Travis showed me six full-sized, customized GMC vans in assorted colors. He suggested that I pick out one and take it for a test drive. He informed me that the color was the only difference in all of them and I selected burgundy.

I drove the van east on I-69 for a few miles, and then I drove back to the dealership.

Travis asked me my opinion, and I told him that the vehicle was nice and rode very well. He said fine and said they would get back with me. I still had no clue as to what was happening.

Why was I asked to test drive that new van? Having no answers, I began to pray on my way back to the jail. "Lord, if Virgil were to provide me this vehicle, You know I will have to turn it down since my family budget would not be able to afford the insurance."

After arriving back at the jail office, my phone rang. "Hello, Mr. Novak, this is Sutton Insurance Company. Virgil is leasing a van for two years from Waldron's GMC, and he is fully insuring the van—and you are being declared the principal driver. You may go over to the dealership and pick up your van. Everything is completed."

Driving back out to Davison, in total awe of God, I picked up His provision that enabled me to minister for another two years. It was a great vehicle and was truly a huge blessing for me and our family. When the two-year lease period was up, it was time to go back to the prayer table again. I owned no other vehicles and was still unable to purchase a vehicle according to our family budget. My only option was to fully trust in the Lord. My pay as a missionary chaplain had increased some, but it was still not enough to afford a car payment along with other family needs.

Our prayer team continued to witness all kinds of answers to prayer, including several miraculous healings and many jail ministry requests. Please note here that our monthly and yearly ministry budget was mentioned to God at every prayer meeting twice each week.

As we added new ministry programs in the jail, our expenses increased. There was a continual need to seek God's provisions for the jail ministry, and we prayed. His Word constantly encouraged our trust that He would provide our needs.

However, considering the many prayers requests that had been affirmatively answered, the proposed budget often found itself with a shortage. Several times we lacked five or ten thousand dollars of meeting the yearly budget. Only twice did we fully meet the budget in Genesee County. Why did God not completely answer our yearly budget requests in our county? I will share why I believe that God could not answer some of those prayer requests.

The budget needs of Genesee County were met; however, God often used Christians from a neighboring county that had been overfunded to subsidize us. Our ministry needs were being met, but not by the Christians who were living and being served in Genesee County.

Why didn't God obtain the funds needed from the Genesee County Christians? My take is that God tried His level best. Wow, is this guy blaspheming God—or what?

No, my friends, God did try to meet our yearly budget, but He needed His people to willingly step up and supply that need. God does need our compliance with a yes. It may be God's will that all persons be saved, but that doesn't mean it will happen. We must submit to Him and be the active part of proclaiming Christ to others. God desires this, but He cannot make it happen if we are unwilling to join Him. God wants and needs us as his partners.

Genesee County consistently had one of highest crime rates in the state, and many Christians even espoused the unloving attitude of "give 'em bread and water and beat 'em twice a day."

These fellow believers simply did not understand that God loves each one of the inmates in the jail and sent His son, Jesus, to die for them also. Many Christians blatantly refuse God's offer to reach out to those behind bars, yet they would gladly lend their support to the homeless shelter in town. It was much easier for our homeless shelter to raise financial support from the Christian community than for the jail ministry.

Crime had personally affected so many people that there was a thinking that we were somehow pampering the criminals in the jail. They were not seeing the bigger picture that God wanted to change these troubled lives from crime to Christ. Often this resulted in the Christian's refusal to financially support God's work at the jail.

Our heavenly Father is a person, and I think He was very disappointed in many of His children with their attitudes of unconcern in reaching the lost in the jail. He tried as hard as He could to change their minds. They just became hard-hearted and unwilling to share God's grace salvation with others bound by the shackles of sin.

My answer for why we could not meet our yearly budget needs was simple: God's people in Genesee County were not willing to do so, and many had hardened their hearts toward getting the Gospel to the inmates. God works through His people, and He really needs us to step forward and make ourselves available to Him including our resources. God was certainly on our side since He desires that all persons, including inmates, be saved (1 Timothy 2:4). My belief is that God's people simply let Him down. As a former police officer, I could understand their feelings since I had observed and arrested criminals and put them in jail. I saw firsthand what they did. But our all-forgiving God loves them and wants to set them free from their bondage of sin and to start a whole new life in Christ. Some believers had become so hard-hearted in Genesee County that they were unable to love others, especially those incarcerated in the county jail.

The jail was filled with spiritual activity, and our Heavenly Father was always present for us to seek Him in prayer. My need for another vehicle became apparent as I was getting closer to the lease termination date. Our prayer team began to ask God again to provide a van for Chaplain Al.

One of our associate chaplains, Bill Stone, was always a faithful prayer warrior on the team. As the men would pray, Bill told us later, God began to speak to him personally. Bill was a retired

General Motors engineering team manager. He said that God had clearly encouraged him to provide a van for me—permanently.

Bill was able to get a good deal on PEP vehicles as a retired GM salaried employee. Supervisory staff were permitted to drive these company-owned vehicles for three to five thousand miles, and then they would evaluate them and turn them in for another one. It was GM's way of having the vehicles expertly reviewed, and it also served as a perk for its managerial employees.

Bill contacted his upline and had a PEP vehicle set aside for me, and he fully insured it as well. God took care of all the details. He informed me that I could drive this vehicle until it had approximately thirty-four thousand miles, and then I was to notify him—and he would get me another low-mileage PEP vehicle to replace it. He did not want me to drive a vehicle that was out of factory warranty.

This began many years of God's provisions of PEP vehicles, including several Pontiac Montanas, a Buick Terraza, and a GMC Safari. These vehicles were provided through Bill's generosity until his death in 1987. The vehicle I was driving when Bill died was later entitled over to me without a word. We kept this vehicle, a 1986 Pontiac Montana, until it had more than 150,000 miles.

The miracles continued, and in 2012, another associate chaplain—one of our faithful supporters—came up to me in the jail before I had even asked for prayer for another vehicle. He handed me a check for forty thousand dollars to replace my aging van. I was completely blown away that God had answered my prayer even before I asked Him.

> Jesus says, "When you are praying, do not heap up empty phrases as the Gentiles do; for they think that they will be heard because of their many words. Do

not be like them, for your Father knows what you need before you ask him." Matthew 6:8 (NRSV)

After reviewing my best purchase options and discounts, I purchased a 2012 Ford Escape. We still have it since I am now retired after thirty-three years of jail ministry.

My son Michael and his family live in Arkansas. They were serving the Lord through Youth With A Mission (YWAM) and were desperately in need of a family vehicle. We drove the Pontiac Montana down and gave it to them for use in their ministry. Michael had been learning skills in auto mechanics and was able to keep this vehicle going all the way up to this day in 2022. His ministry had transitioned from YWAM into Ecclesia Christian College, and after many years, Michael is now the president of this Christian liberal arts work-learning college. This college, where a student can graduate free of debt, is located near Springdale, Arkansas, and online at ecollege.edu. God supplied us with a vehicle and moved it forward to assist others who serve Him.

Why do I boast about how wonderful our God really is? The stories of God's continual provisions that I have shared with you are undeniably true. God is the provider of our needs (Jehovah Jireh), and I pray that my story will be an encouragement for you to pray about everything.

> "Be anxious for nothing, but in everything by prayer and supplication, with thanksgiving, let your requests be made known to God;" Philippians 4:6 (NKJV)

> "You did not choose me, but I chose you and appointed you so that you might go and bear

fruit—fruit that will last—and so that whatever you ask in my name the Father will give you." John 15:16 (NIV)

Needs and wants are different, and God is in the needs business. He is always available through our one and only Mediator, Jesus Christ.

"For there is one God, and one mediator between God and men, the man Christ Jesus." 1 Timothy 2:5 (KJV)

Thanks be to our one true God and Father—and praise be to Jesus Christ, our Savior, Mediator, and Lord! Amen.

CHAPTER 39

"Al, I Got Your Back"

In early 2013, I was diagnosed with an inguinal hernia. The hernia-repair surgeon required that I have a stress test prior to the repair. The cardiologist gave me a nuclear stress test and an echocardiogram with a bubble. The stress test revealed some slight abnormality, and the echocardiogram revealed that I had a small hole in my heart. I had never experienced any heart issues of any kind—or any symptoms or signs related to any heart issues.

This abnormality resulted in my cardiologist performing two test procedures: a trans-esophageal echocardiogram (TEE) and a heart catheterization to search for the root cause of this small irregularity. Both procedures were scheduled for the same day at McLaren Hospital in Flint. The TEE was first.

I was put asleep by an anesthesiologist, and they placed a tube down my throat. It would send sound waves from the back of my heart to show if there were any problems from that point of view. As I was coming out of the anesthesia and waking up from the TEE, I was in a mind-altering state of euphoria and imagined to be in the most beautiful place of perfect peace and rest. I said, "This stuff is really good! Can I take some home with me?"

Everybody in the room burst out laughing. The anesthesiologist said that I could not take some home, and he chuckled along with the others.

This made me realize for the first time how drugs could make you feel like you are in an oasis of perfect peace and why one could be so attracted to feeling like this—even illegally. Everyone clamors for peace within as did the people with whom I hung out with prior to knowing the Lord of peace.

> "Now may the Lord of peace Himself grant you His peace at all times and in every way [that peace and spiritual well-being that comes to those who walk with Him, regardless of life's circumstances]. The Lord be with you all." 2 Thessalonians 3:16 (AMP)

When the TEE was completed, my cardiologist informed me that my heart seemed very strong. I most likely would not even require one stent. Even though the test disclosed that my heart was strong, the doctor was still concerned about the slight abnormality that had surfaced in my prior stress test. He asked me if I wanted to continue and do the next scheduled procedure of a heart catheterization. He told me that an operating room was reserved down the hall and ready to go, but it was up to me.

Developing a genuine trust in my doctor, I asked him what he would do if it was him. He said even though the TEE was affirming, he felt that the heart catheterization procedure would disclose another view of my heart condition, which might give them some additional information. If it was him, he would do the next procedure to confirm the condition of the heart.

Trusting in his expertise, I submitted to the procedure. I was transported down the hall to another room and placed back under anesthesia. The heart catheterization was a much more extensive procedure, and they injected a contrast dye into the heart area, which revealed a clear picture of my heart from a frontal view.

There were no euphoric experiences awakening from the second anesthesia. Upon returning to consciousness, my cardiologist, Dr. Predeteanu, who speaks with a Romanian accent, said, "Meester Novak, why are you alive?"

In a reviving stupor, his words seemed very puzzling. I said, "What?"

He said, "We do not know why you are alive."

I responded, "By God's grace, I believe."

He chuckled and said, "No, Meester Novak, let me show you!" He pulled a computer screen next to my surgical bed and placed it directly in front of me. He pointed to the screen and said this picture shows a 95 percent blockage of a main artery, which is commonly called the "widow-maker."

I said, "Did you say 90 percent blocked!"

He said, "No, Meester Novak, I said 95 percent blocked!" He showed me a second photo. My second main artery was 95 percent blocked. The snakelike vein was dammed up and bulging in one area of the tributary it followed. He showed me a third picture of my heart. "This is your third main artery flowing from your heart, and it also is 95 percent blocked."

The question that he asked me was a valid question. Why was I alive with these three main artery blockages? My answer also was correct in stating that it was by God's grace. Most of the blood flowing to your main organs are pumped through these three main arteries.

He showed me another amazing thing that had taken place in my body. The picture revealed a bunch of tiny veins all around and below my heart. Dr. Predeteanu told me that I was not born with them. My body had produced them recently, forcing an alternate blood flow to my organs, but they were not there from the beginning. He said the feeder veins were basically keeping me alive. I knew unquestionably that God was responsible for producing those feeder veins. His grace was keeping me alive, but scientifically speaking, I was also a primary candidate for triple-bypass open-heart surgery.

There were two options set before me: (1) do nothing (most likely resulting in sudden death with no symptoms) or (2) triple-bypass open-heart surgery (hopefully extending my life). Yes, those feeder veins were keeping me alive, but those blood passages were insufficient for a continued normal life.

Choosing door number two and staying alive through open-heart surgery was my final decision. My cardiologist connected me with a heart surgeon, and a hurried surgical plan was placed on the docket. Within a week, all the necessary procedures were set in place. I was scheduled for open-heart surgery on September 12, 2013, at 8:00 a.m. at McLaren Hospital.

Being a jail chaplain for twenty-eight years had connected me with many Christians and churches. Monthly newsletters and reports linked me with more than 250 churches in the county sharing ministry opportunities and support opportunities. My oldest son, Jeff, was very active with his church in Virginia. Michael, our second born, worked on staff with the YWAM program in Arkansas and was in contact with thousands of pastors around the world. My youngest son Joey was a pastor of a Presbyterian church in Ithaca, Michigan. Jenni, our eldest daughter, was a faithful prayer warrior, and Carmie, our youngest, was an event coordinator for a large church in North Canton, Ohio.

All five of our children, their spouses, our grandchildren, their friends, their churches, and a host of friends on Facebook, the many churches on my email list, all thirty-three associate chaplains who assisted at the jail and their churches, 150 jail ministry volunteers and their churches and our home office family in Grand Rapids, thirty-five other county jail chaplains, and their associate chaplains were asked to pray. Talk about an amazing prayer team of support? I really had it!

The best way to share with you how God answered the many prayers that were being offered for me began on the morning of the surgery. I was scheduled to be at McLaren Hospital at five thirty in the morning for surgical preparation. Open-heart surgery, even though it is quite common, is considered the most serious surgery performed in the hospital—even greater than brain surgery. The surgical procedure was scheduled to begin at eight o'clock.

Before leaving for the hospital that morning, my protocol was to shower with a special antibacterial soap and shampoo. During my shower, I began to reflect on what was about to happen to me. I started to get scared and shaky inside, and an extraordinary anxiety took over.

Gathering all my stuff after the shower, I got into our car. I asked Terri to drive as an increasing fearfulness continued to overshadow me. Halfway to the hospital, God took control. As I sat in my car seat, I physically experienced two arms gently embrace me from the back with a big hug around my entire upper body.

In my spirit, God clearly spoke in my ear as I felt His arms hugging me. He said, "Al, I got your back!" The experience was real and not in my imagination even though I could not explain it. There was no making up a story, and His life-changing presence at that moment became as real to me as Saul (Paul) on the road to Damascus had encountered Jesus (Acts 9).

At that very moment, a total and complete calm fell over me. The shuddering that I had been experiencing completely ceased, and my body became very relaxed. With confidence, there was an absolute certainty in my spirit, and all the fear and anxieties had left me. I began to joke around with Terri, as my whole countenance had changed. She noticed immediately the difference. I told her that God had given me a hug and told me that He had my back. After arriving at the hospital, my upbeat joking and calmness continued with the hospital attendants as I moved along through the preparations for the surgery.

I knew for certain that I had nothing to worry about since God had told me that He had my back. How could anyone worry when God takes charge of things? He was answering the prayers of all those who had been praying for me. There was no reason to worry since He has unlimited resources to look after my heart surgery and the post-op healing.

Amazingly, every presurgical and postsurgical test was passed with an A plus. During the surgery procedure, the patient is placed on a table. The chest is cut open, the lungs collapse, and a ventilator is ascribed until all the repairs are made to the heart. The ventilator is usually connected for four to twenty-four hours after the heart surgery is completed, but mine was removed in one hour. Oh, yeah, did I tell you that God had my back!

Being placed in the intensive care unit (ICU), awaiting to regain consciousness, my eyes began to open. There was a nurse standing next to my bed, and her name tag read: "Hope."

As I was coming out of the anesthesia, I said, "Are you an angel?"

She smiled and said, "No."

I said, "You must be an angel with a name like Hope."

She laughed. She became a very special caregiver to me. She had two patients to care for, but I remember her being there all the time to help me. God really did have my back as I moved closer toward full recovery.

The morning after my open-heart surgery, Hope asked if I would like to take a short walk.

I said, "Sure!"

She got a wheelchair and placed my two draining tube units, which were collecting fluids from my heart, onto the wheelchair.

She rolled out the IV bag that was replacing fluids in my body, helped me stand up, as I grabbed the wheelchair handles from the rear. She informed me that we would walk very slowly for just a short time.

The ICU had three sections that contained a walkway around each unit of maybe thirty rooms. We began to walk around the first unit down the hallway. Hope continued to ask if I was all right. I told her I was fine as we continued to walk and talk about family and other things, including my faith story. She told me all about her family, and we continued walking. After completing the walk around the first unit, we approached a return hallway that would lead us back to my room.

She asked if I wanted to continue walking, and I told her that I did. We continued walking and talking all the way around the second unit and came to a second return hallway that would lead us back to my room. She asked if I was tired and wanted to return to my bed. I told her that I felt good, and we continued to walk.

As we completed the entire walk around all three sections, Hope helped me get back into my bed. She said, "Al, you are the first person I have seen in thirty years of nursing who has walked around all three units the first day after open-heart surgery."

I told her all about God having my back and how thousands of people were praying for me. Every postoperative test that I was given had very positive results.

After two days in the ICU, I was taken up to a surgical floor. Hope walked me up to my new floor, and she began to cry. I asked her why she was crying. She said that my personal care most likely would be reduced on the medical floor unlike that received in ICU. She had truly become my angel of care and well-being, and we became great friends.

She was correct, and the healing process became more challenging for me on that floor. There is always limited staffing on general medical floors and less availability of assistance. My condition was getting better by the hour, and they subsequently released me from the hospital in less than five days.

After returning home and adjusting to the healing process, which is not a piece of cake by any means—and by God's grace—I was able to continue my three-mile walks after only two weeks. My insurance company suggested that they would like me to be their poster child (senior) for open-heart surgery due to my phenomenal surgical success. I declined their offer since I knew that God alone was the reason for such success.

So, how did God answer the prayers of all those who were praying for me? God gave me a big hug and told me that He had my back, assuring me of His personal oversight, surgical guidance, and full charge of the recovery process. He watched over the entire surgical procedure and guided the hands of the heart surgeon and those in the aftercare process. He provided a special nurse to help me through my initial recovery and granted me a super quick, total, and complete healing process. When God takes charge, there is nothing to worry about—period!

Thank You, dear Father, for all those who prayed for me and how You answered each of those requests with a yes. I am truly grateful, humbled, and blessed by Your personal attention, life altering hug, and assurances of love for me. I love you so much as I pray these things in the wonderful name of Jesus. Amen.

CHAPTER 40
Back to Intimacy

Walking through each doorway of my spiritual journey made me long for more of God. This longing continued throughout my life and persuaded me to chase after an intimate relationship with our heavenly Father. Traveling in the byways of religion began my process of learning about God. The priests and teachers of my youth, Bible instructors and pastors along the way, my personal and systematic studies, reading Christian literature, and sensing God's leading kept gnawing away at my heart that there must be a deeper spiritual connection with God.

My first intimate contact with God began when I cried out and asked Jesus to be my Savior. This initial act of faith tethered me in a personal relationship with God through His Son. No one can come to God but through Jesus says the scripture. The door to intimacy with our heavenly Father was flung open to me.

As my faith developed through early childhood, spiritual growth continued thanks to a variety of Christian denominations. These are listed in the following order of attendance: Roman Catholic, Community Church, Lutheran CA, Lutheran Missouri

Synod, Regular Baptist, Independent Baptist, IFCA Bible Churches, Regular Baptist Churches, and Presbyterian. Learning about God in all these churches left a longing in my heart to know Him more intimately like Jesus in John 17 had prayed that we do. Chasing intimacy was afoot as my spiritual journey moved forward.

For thirty-three years I shared jail ministry and preached at hundreds of different churches and denominations in Genesee County; God opened my eyes to something. I discovered that God had a remnant of genuine believers in every church that love Him with all their hearts. These I would declare to you are the truly born-again children of God and not the many who claim to be a Christian.

Yes, my journey from religion subsequently led me to a re-birth in the spiritual realm. Then some fellow Christians introduced me to legalism. It was there that I learned separation from others, including fellow believers. Practicing these freshly learned faux-Protestant positions kept me a distance away from God. Studying more of God's Word and His grace teachings enabled me to struggle out of that trap. Ah, yes, grace! What a wonderful word. It means that God just accepts us as is. No works, no merit, no stress, no traditions, no religious practices, but just as we are. He says, "I love you more."

God's Word speaks to us about this amazing grace of God:

> "For by grace are ye saved through faith; and that not of yourselves: it is the gift of God: Not of works, lest any man should boast." Ephesians 2:8–9 (KJV)

A great song entitled "Just As I Am" was always sung at the conclusion of a Billy Graham Crusade and often at other church evangelistic services after an invitation to receive Christ was given. It goes like this:

Just as I am, without one plea, but that Thy blood was shed for me, and that Thou bid'st me come to Thee, O Lamb of God, I come! I come!

Just as I am and waiting not, to rid my soul of one dark blot, to Thee whose blood can cleanse each spot, O Lamb of God, I come! I come!

Just as I am, tho tossed about with many a conflict, many a doubt, fightings and fears within, without, O Lamb of God, I come! I come!

Just as I am, poor, wretched, blind; sight, riches, healing of the mind, yea, all I need, in Thee to find, O Lamb of God, I come! I come! Just as I am, Thou wilt receive, Wilt welcome, pardon, cleanse, relieve; because Thy promise I believe, O Lamb of God, I come! I come!

After learning, enjoying, and bathing in God's grace, a new mandate was placed on me to perform for God. I entitled this as performance theology. So, what does performance theology mean?

God expects us to perform for Him, correct? God is not happy with you until you are carrying out all your Christian duties and responsibilities. My beloved reader, that is very far from the heart of God. The truth is that He does not want our performance at all; He simply wants us on His team. He wants us to be available to Him with no agendas or strings attached, allowing Him to perform through us. With that understanding in mind, we certainly cannot take any credit since He is doing all the work. Therefore, He should get all the honor, praise, and glory as He alone deserves it.

Performance theology is another attempt of Satan to rob God of His glory. There is no performance in simply offering yourself to God as a living sacrifice and follower of Jesus; you are merely making yourself available to Him!

> "I beseech you therefore, brethren, by the mercies of God, that ye present your bodies a living sacrifice, holy, acceptable unto God, which is your reasonable service." Romans 12:1 (KJV)

Bypassing the customary religious life protocols, I found myself right back where it all began in an intimate relationship with God. Basically, my whole life was chasing after this intimacy that I experienced from the very beginning and finding spiritual satisfaction during the journey. Intimacy became the resting place to true inner peace and spiritual fulfillment. It is the place where I can hug my heavenly Dad and sit comfortably and lovingly on His lap. Have you ever wanted to sit there secure in His presence? Our Heavenly Father has His arms outstretched to lift you up on His lap today and to give you a great big hug. His desire is to hold you tightly, embrace you in His arms, and begin a deeper intimate relationship with Him. He is waiting for you!

Conclusion

God sincerely desires to be closer with us in a deeper loving relationship. My hope is that chasing intimacy may become a new spiritual longing for you. Identifying and fleeing the traps of traditional religion can be a steppingstone toward Him. The many benefits include spiritual satisfaction throughout your journey. Jesus considered it a major priority in His life and would often stop during His daily ministries and go up into the mountains to be alone with His Father and pray. Jesus chased intimacy with His Father, and He desired to sit in His Dad's lap as His loving Son. This is something for us to follow because—through our faith and trust in Christ—we are God's children also.

Religion's legalism, dogmatism, formalism, and performance theology left me dry and thirsty to know God in a deeper way. Religion, in my opinion, is like the outside door that often leads to pious servitude and performance for God, but little satisfaction.

My spiritual journey led me from a presupposed religious vocation into living a basic moral life, getting married, having children, and pursuing a career as a police officer. My police career led me down a road filled with many potholes. The crucial change of inviting Jesus Christ to be my personal Savior enabled me to find genuine peace within and a real relationship with God. Jesus did say that He was the way, the truth, and the life and that no person can come to God except through Him. The wages of sin are death, but for those who believe in Christ, their resurrection from this earthly death to life eternal is promised in the scriptures when the trump of God is sounded. My hope is to be alive when this occurs; however, the promise of a future life in Paradise with the Lord is something to anticipate.

> "For the Lord himself will come down from heaven with a commanding shout, with the voice of the archangel, and with the trumpet call of God. First, the believers who have died will rise from their graves. Then, together with them, we who are still alive and remain on the earth will be caught up in the clouds to meet the Lord in the air. Then we will be with the Lord forever. So encourage each other with these words." 1 Thessalonians 4: 13–18 (NLT)

Randy Young, a former fellow police officer, shared with me the gospel and offered me an invitation to receive Jesus Christ. By faith, I placed all my trust in Him—and my life was changed forever—not only my life but the lives of my family to follow. Hearing the Gospel is what I needed, and knowing God intimately became the journey throughout my life. Had he not shared with me that offer, I and my family's heritage might still be lost in sin.

> "So then faith comes by hearing, and hearing by the word of God." Romans 10:17 (NKJV)

The Gospel of Christ that Randy proclaimed to me is clearly found in the scriptures:

> "Moreover, brethren, I declare to you the Gospel ... that Christ died for our sins according to the scriptures, and that He was buried, and that He

rose again the third day according to the scriptures, and that He was seen by Cephas, then by the twelve. After that He was seen by over five hundred brethren at once." 1 Corinthians 15 (NKJV)

Receiving Christ will change your life, but God will do the changing. His amazing grace will make all things in your life brand new:

"Therefore if any man be in Christ, he is a new creature: old things are passed away; behold, all things are become new." 2 Corinthians 5:17 (KJV)

Finding intimacy with our heavenly Father is like seeing something with blurred vision that suddenly clears up. I imagined myself living at the time of Jesus and standing in the healing aisle. I am thirty-eighth in line, and Jesus had been healing all day long everyone who came by faith. When I finally arrive at the front of the line, Jesus speaks to the ailing crowd and says that He must go and be alone with His Father—and He heads out to some remote location.

If Jesus thought it was more important to take time for intimacy with His Father, then I—as God's child—should do likewise. Chasing intimacy enabled my vision to clear up and seek what Jesus sought. This led me to read books that shared personal journeys from other Christians who had sought after the same. These Christian books developed in me a lifetime pursuit and thus became the title of this book.

Some great books of testimonies, stories, journals, and studies that helped point me toward chasing intimacy are:

1. *Experiencing God: Knowing and Doing the Will of God* (Henry Blackaby and Claude King). I spent six months

journaling through this book in a group study at church. This study enabled me to discover a deeper sense of God's presence and activity in my life, leading me toward Him.

2. *Intimacy with the Almighty* (Charles R. Swindoll). I have read this book many times. It is a short read. This book will take you on an intriguing journey into deeper awareness of God. Four disciplines are suggested in the book. (1) Simplify your life. (2) Be silent with God. (3) Find solitude with Him. (4) Totally surrender to Him. These disciplines are not generally easy, but the outcomes are so worth the chase as one intimately embraces Him.

3. *The Practice of the Presence of God* (Brother Lawrence). This book contains conversations and letters from a Roman Catholic monk in France in the 1600s. Brother Lawrence found out that he could enjoy the presence of God even while he cleaned the pots and pans in the kitchen. It is a spiritual eye-opener that everyone can practice His presence whenever and wherever possible. Brother Lawrence says, "There is not in the world a kind of life more sweet and delightful than that of a continual conversation with God." Setting Him before us while sitting in His holy presence permits us to have the special intimacy with God that we all desire. It becomes a habitual, silent, and private conversation of the soul with God.

The eleventh, twelfth, and thirteenth letters in Brother Lawrence's book contain traditional Roman Catholic teachings about suffering for one's sins. The scriptures teach that Jesus suffered and died for me. Oh, yes, I deserve to suffer, but He took all my punishment. He was beaten and suffered death on a cross, and He paid my penalty for sin—and then He said that it was finished. The only scriptural response that I can find in the scriptures is for us to offer Him the sacrifice of praise. I disagree with Brother

Lawrence's position on the need for personal suffering for sin since the scriptures say that Jesus paid it all—and I owe it all to Him. Praise be to Him! There is a scripture that speaks of our continual sacrifice as an offering of praise:

> "Through Jesus, therefore, let us continually offer to God a sacrifice of praise—the fruit of lips that openly profess his name." Hebrews 13:15 (NIV)

4. *Beholding and Becoming* (Jerry Coulter). This book is out of print but used copies might be found online. It shows believers how to fellowship with Jesus Christ in the spirit—through our imaginations—since we think in images and pictures. After all, we are body, soul, and spirit. Galatians 5:16 (KJV) says that we are to "walk in the spirit." What does it mean to walk in the spirit and not fulfill the lust of the flesh? How can we behold and become like Christ according to 2 Corinthians 3:18 (NKJV)?

5. *Relational Christianity* (Reverend Steve Meeks). Pastor Meeks takes his congregation into a journey of cultivating the presence of God by using gardening as an illustration. His presence secures you, purifies you, works through you, and guides you. We find victory not by facing personal darkness but by turning to the Lord's intimate brightness.

6. Other books were of great assistance to me and provided practical applications that enabled me to continue the chase. Some of these books may be theologically questioned, but please do not throw the baby out with the bathwater. Some of the books recommended below utilize scriptures that will point you toward Him. Seedsowers.com has the

following list of books that can be very helpful in chasing intimacy:

- *Experiencing the Depths of Jesus Christ* (Jeanne Guyon)
- *Living Close to God* (Gene Edwards)
- *Practicing the Presence* (Brother Lawrence and Frank Laubach)
- *The Seeking Heart* (Francois Fenelon)
- *The Spiritual Guide* (Michael Molinos)
- *The Inward Journey* (Gene Edwards)
- *Union with God* (Madame Guyon)

Koinonia is a New Testament Greek word that means "supernatural withness." It signifies association, communion, fellowship, or even intercourse. When people turn from the things of God and becomes preoccupied with God Himself, they enjoy God "withness." That is what this book is primarily all about.

My prayer is that *Chasing Intimacy* will result in a deep, daily "koinonia" or close encounter and inner abiding with the only true God. Jesus prayed that knowing Him (His heavenly Father, the one true God) and Jesus, God's Son and Messiah, the anointed One, intimately is eternal life:

> "And this is eternal life, that they may know you, the only true God, and Jesus Christ whom you have sent" (John 17:3 NASB)

In *Relational Christianity,* Reverend Steve Meeks explains that silence and stillness will sow seeds that will grow in your heart and produce the fragrance of His presence with you. Get alone, get still, and get quiet before God.

"Be still (*or cease striving*) and know that I am God."
Psalm 46:10 (KJV)

Chasing Intimacy will continue throughout your life until it ends in death but the moment you partake of that first intimate connection with God, a whole new abundant life of spiritual satisfaction shall begin. Blessings and joy on your journey.

The End

About the Author

Al Novak served as a police officer for seventeen years. After accepting Jesus Christ as Savior and Lord, he served as a jail chaplain for thirty-three years until retiring in 2018. He and his wife Terri have five adult children and twelve grandchildren. They reside in Flint, Michigan.

Made in United States
Orlando, FL
30 January 2024